The Hoodwinking of Madeline

AND OTHER ESSAYS ON KEATS'S POEMS

JACK STILLINGER

The Hoodwinking
of Madeline

AND OTHER ESSAYS
ON KEATS'S POEMS

UNIVERSITY OF ILLINOIS PRESS

Urbana   Chicago   London

୬ଚ   If you and Poe
      and I and Keats
      went on a picnic,
      we could pack some goodies,
      jump in the old balloon,
      and take off.

      But at some point,
      seeing the world recede so fast,
      Keats and I would get nervous,
      and, luckily having brought our parachutes,
      would return to earth,
      where, still in the picnic spirit,
      we'd run and throw the football
      and watch you and Poe
      become a tiny speck in the sky.

      What's a nice girl like you
      doing in a balloon
      with an unsavory character like Poe?
      Come join us!
      We need someone to center the ball.

৵ঙ Preface

With the exception of the first part of Appendix III, the pieces collected here were written over the last ten years. My main reason for bringing them together, apart from a desire to make them more readily available to students (for whom, rather than scholars, the volume is primarily intended), is that they all proceed from the same view of what Keats's poems are principally about, and relate to one another in expounding that view. The idea is most plainly stated in three sentences near the beginning of the essay on the odes: "[Keats's] significant poems center on a single basic problem, the mutability inherent in nature and human life, and openly or in disguise they debate the pros and cons of a single hypothetical solution, transcendence of earthly limitations by means of the visionary imagination. . . . Keats came to learn that this kind of imagination was a false lure, inadequate to the needs of the problem, and in the end he traded it for the naturalized imagination, embracing experience and process as his own and man's chief good. His honesty in treating the problem and his final opting for the natural world, where all the concrete images of poetry come from and where melodies impinge on 'the sensual ear' or not at all, are what, more than anything else, guarantee his place 'among the English Poets.'" I do not for a minute believe that Keats's magnificent achievement in poetry can be explained by any such simple notion as I have set down here and in the essays. But I have come to think that the idea has a rightness and a usefulness *toward* understanding the individual works that earlier and some contemporary accounts seem to lack.

The previously published essays originally appeared as follows: "The Order of Poems in Keats's First Volume" in *Philological Quarterly,* XLVIII (1969), 92–101; "On the Interpretation of *Endymion:* The Comedian as the Letter E" in *Romantic and Victorian: Studies in Memory of William H. Marshall,* ed. W. Paul Elledge and Richard L. Hoffman (Rutherford, N.J.: Fairleigh Dickinson University Press, 1971); "Keats and Romance: The 'Reality' of *Isabella"* in *Studies in English Literature,* VIII (1968), 593–605; "The Hoodwinking of Madeline: Skepticism in *The Eve of St. Agnes"* in *Studies in Philology,* LVIII (1961), 533–555; "The Meaning of 'Poor Cheated Soul' in *The Eve of Saint Mark"* in *English Language Notes,* V (1968), 193–196; and "Imagination and Reality in the Odes" as the introduction to *Twentieth Century Interpretations of Keats's Odes* (Englewood Cliffs, N.J.: Prentice-Hall, Inc., 1968). Section III of "Keats, Wordsworth, and 'Romanticism'" incorporates several paragraphs of my introduction to *William Wordsworth: Selected Poems and Prefaces* (Boston: Houghton Mifflin Co., 1965). Appendixes II and IV were first published in *Studies in Bibliography,* XVI (1963), 207–212, and XXII (1969), 255–258. Appendix III reproduces much of a note in *PMLA,* LXXIII (1958), 447–448, and the appendix in *Twentieth Century Interpretations of Keats's Odes.* I am grateful to the editors and publishers of these journals and books for permission to reprint the various pieces. All have been at least slightly revised to correct occasional inaccuracies and eliminate repetitions of phrasing. I have allowed some larger repetitions to remain—the recurring references to a few key passages (e.g., Keats's letter to Bailey on the imagination, the *King Lear* sonnet, certain lines from *Sleep and Poetry* and *Endymion*) and the tracing of Keats's entire career in both "The Hoodwinking of Madeline" and "Imagination and Reality in the Odes"—because I felt that these were essential to the argument in each place. " 'The Heart and Nature of Man' in *Hyperion, Lamia,* and *The Fall of Hyperion,*" "Keats, Wordsworth, and 'Romanticism' " (except for section III), and Appendix I have not been published before (nor has the Epilogue).

The Index contains the names of sixty-five Keats scholars and critics, and I have been influenced by all of them, even those I most disagree with. I owe a special debt to the teaching and writings of Walter Jackson Bate, Douglas Bush, Walter H. Evert, David Perkins, and Earl R. Wasserman, and wish to record my thanks to them. The lines following the title page, which originally appeared in *Prairie Schooner,* XLII (1968), 60–61, under the title "On Being Reminded of Keats on Every Other Page of Professor Nina Baym's Poe Article," serve here as a dedication of sorts, and also as one more interpretation of Keats. The Epilogue is an interpretation of me.

Contents

The Order of Poems in Keats's First Volume   1

On the Interpretation of *Endymion:* The Comedian as the Letter E   14

Keats and Romance: The "Reality" of *Isabella*   31

"The Heart and Nature of Man" in *Hyperion, Lamia,* and *The Fall of Hyperion*   46

The Hoodwinking of Madeline: Skepticism in *The Eve of St. Agnes*   67

The Meaning of "Poor Cheated Soul" in *The Eve of Saint Mark*   94

Imagination and Reality in the Odes   99

Keats, Wordsworth, and "Romanticism"   120

Appendix   I: Keats's Letter to Bailey on the Imagination   151

Appendix II: The Text of *The Eve of St. Agnes*   158

Appendix III: Who Says What to Whom at the End of *Ode on a Grecian Urn?*   167

Appendix IV: The Text of *Ode on Indolence*   174

Epilogue   179

Index   181

The Order of
Poems in Keats's
First Volume

Although the chronological ordering of a writer's works, even in selections, is undoubtedly the most expedient arrangement for general study, we always run the danger, in any too strict adherence to chronology, of losing or overlooking certain effects intended by the writer in the original presentation of his works to the public. In the second edition of *Lyrical Ballads* (1800), for example, the conclusion of the famous Preface, in which Wordsworth rather grandly asserts his "claim to the approbation of the public" for offering "a species of poetry . . . well adapted to interest mankind permanently, and likewise important in the multiplicity and quality of its moral relations," is followed (after a blank leaf) by *Expostulation and Reply,* which begins:

> "Why, William, on that old grey stone,
> Thus for length of half a day,
> Why, William, sit you thus alone,
> And dream your time away?"

Obviously we miss a fine rise of irony (and have missed Wordsworth's essential playfulness in the poem) when the Preface is relegated to the back of the volume and the poem is placed and read either chronologically among the compositions of the spring of 1798 or, in Wordsworth's own later classification, among the "Poems of Sentiment and Reflection." The final two poems of Wordsworth's edition of 1807 were *Elegiac Stanzas, Suggested by a Picture of Peele Castle* and the *Intimations* ode (then simply titled *Ode*). The effect of passing from the conclusion of the one,

I

"Not without hope we suffer and we mourn," to the opening of the other,

> There was a time when meadow, grove, and stream,
> The earth, and every common sight,
> To me did seem
> Apparell'd in celestial light,
> The glory and the freshness of a dream.
> It is not now as it has been of yore . . .

is of course entirely lost by Wordsworth's later separating of the poems in the section called "Epitaphs and Elegiac Pieces" and by our own placing of them in their respective chronological positions for 1806 and 1802–04.

In Keats's *Lamia* volume (1820) there are several such juxtapositions or sequences having critical significance. *Ode to Psyche*, ending on a seemingly positive note with the speaker's declaration that he will build a temple to Psyche in his mind—"A rosy sanctuary . . . With all the gardener Fancy e'er could feign"— is immediately followed by the poem *Fancy* ("Ever let the Fancy roam, / Pleasure never is at home"), which offers at once both expansion and qualification of the idea at the conclusion of the ode. The last of the shorter poems in the volume, *To Autumn* and *Ode on Melancholy,* are intimately related in theme and imagery. In time of composition, however, *Fancy* preceded *Ode to Psyche* by four months during which Keats wrote *The Eve of St. Agnes, La Belle Dame sans Merci,* and several sonnets; *Ode on Melancholy* preceded *To Autumn* by another four months in which Keats wrote *Otho the Great* and *Lamia,* among other works. And whatever the explanation, it is surely no accident that *Ode to a Nightingale* and *Ode on a Grecian Urn* were printed before instead of (as they seem to have been written) after *Ode to Psyche,* in the same volume.[1]

---

[1] For a brief statement on the order of poems in the *Lamia* volume, see "Imagination and Reality in the Odes," below, the last paragraph of section II.

While it should not surprise anyone that poets do frequently give serious thought to the arrangement of their poems, the fact is that we almost never consider either their intentions or the effects critically. In particular, there does not seem to be in print any definitive statement concerning the arrangement, or order, of poems in Keats's first volume, published in March 1817. Critics do, of course, characterize the volume as a whole, pointing out lushness, sentimentality, the absence of symbol, a concomitant tendency toward prosiness, and the like; but they seldom suggest why Keats printed one poem before or after another. The readiest explanation for this neglect is that biographers and biographically oriented critics, naturally unwilling to discuss the poems twice—at both composition and publication—have almost universally chosen to treat the poems chronologically according to composition. Another explanation is simply the fact that a number of the poems, lacking sufficient merit or interest, are often ignored altogether. There is obviously still another explanation, however—the possibly widespread feeling that a rationale for Keats's arrangement does not (and never did) exist. "It is difficult to understand what principle guided Keats in their selection," writes Ernest de Selincourt of certain of the poems.[2] And, investigating the implications of Keats's own epigraph for the volume—

> What more felicity can fall to creature,
> Than to enjoy delight with liberty
> (Spenser, *Muiopotmos,* ll. 209–210)

—J. R. Caldwell gives several paragraphs to showing that "wildness and profusion and lack of design distinguished Keats in his own day."[3] Writers have, like Dorothy Hewlett, seen a pattern

[2] Ernest de Selincourt, ed., *The Poems of John Keats,* 5th ed. (London, 1926), p. 388.

[3] James Ralston Caldwell, *John Keats' Fancy* (Ithaca, 1945), pp. 26-28. Caldwell cites, among other contemporaries, George Felton Mathew, who, reviewing *Poems* in the *European Magazine* for May 1817 (LXXI, 435),

of "poetic growth" in the volume.[4] But I believe W. J. Bate is
virtually alone in considering the matter from Keats's own point
of view: "By the first of January [1817] the poems were assembled for the press. He had been thinking about the arrangement.
He would begin it with 'I stood tiptoe,' knowing that something
fairly good was needed to catch the eye. . . . But otherwise Keats
thought it best to put the earliest and poorest poems first . . .
[to] allow the reader to feel a progressive rise."[5] The speculation

remarks that Keats "seems to have a principle, that plan and arrangement
are prejudicial to natural poetry." Similarly, Josiah Conder begins his notice
in the *Eclectic Review* for September 1817 (new ser., VIII, 267), "There is
perhaps no description of publication that comes before us, in which there
is . . . less of what is emphatically denominated *thought,* than in a volume
of miscellaneous poems. . . . what should we think of a person's pro-
fessedly sitting down to write prose . . . without any definite object but the
amusement afforded by the euphonous collocation of sentences?" Mathew
and Conder are probably thinking of the lack of "plan" and "object"
primarily in individual poems, especially in *I stood tip-toe* and *Sleep and
Poetry,* but their observations provide a background for statements like de
Selincourt's implying that Keats selected the poems and ordered them
almost at random.

[4] Dorothy Hewlett, *A Life of John Keats,* 2nd ed., revised (New York,
1950), p. 76. She is not describing Keats's own plan, but is simply observing
that poems like the Chapman's Homer sonnet and *Sleep and Poetry* represent an accession of maturity over "the callow imitation of Spenser and the
'square-toed' eighteenth-century lines to Hope."

[5] Walter Jackson Bate, *John Keats* (Cambridge, Mass., 1963), p. 141.
"Or," Bate continues, "he may have been thinking . . . simply of grouping
the poems in a way that seemed inevitable to him—in a roughly chronological sequence." This is not a bad idea. But three-fourths of the datable
poems in the volume were composed during 1816, and half during the last
six months of the year. Keats's apologetic note on the verso of the Dedication leaf—"The Short Pieces in the middle of the Book, as well as some of
the Sonnets, were written at an earlier period than the rest of the Poems"—
is probably best read as making a simple distinction between the recent
work of 1816, especially the latter months, and that of "an earlier period,"
mainly 1815 but perhaps also including the first months of 1816, during
which the "Short Pieces" from *To Some Ladies* through *Woman! when I
behold thee* and at least the sonnets *Written on the Day that Mr. Leigh
Hunt Left Prison* and *O Solitude!* were composed. "Roughly chronological

is valid so far. What is wanted, however, is an explanation of some kind of thematic development to go along with the "progressive rise." It has long been obvious that Keats's dominant preoccupation in these poems is poetry itself, with a centering on the question of whether he can and should be a poet. Nearly everything in the volume is related to this question, and I think there is a chartable progress from hesitancy to affirmation that explains both the order and the relatedness of the poems. It is the main purpose of this essay briefly and in rather mechanical fashion to outline this development and thereby justify the arrangement.

In one sense, practically every idea and motif in *Poems* of 1817 can be seen as following from the opening proposition of the dedicatory sonnet *To Leigh Hunt, Esq.*:[6]

> Glory and loveliness have passed away.

"No wreathed incense . . . No crowd of nymphs . . . Pan is no longer sought": it is an early version of *Ode to Psyche,* lines 37–41, and the first of many evidences in his work that Keats viewed his own time as an age much more sophisticated and complicated than any that had gone before, an age from which "cold philosophy" had banished fairies and gods, myth and religion. (In dealing critically with poets who lived 150 years ago, we must con-

sequence" better applies to the section of seventeen sonnets, but even here poems from the last five months of 1816 are distributed throughout the group (Sonnets I, VI, VIII, IX, XI–XVI). The three epistles are in chronological order.

[6] In the present account, purporting to describe Keats's intentions as well as the effects of his arrangement of poems, it does not matter that this dedicatory sonnet was the last piece composed (apparently extempore, in February 1817). Keats obviously had the idea and the predominant images in mind through much of the preceding year. As a justification for my approach here, which is to treat the poems *as if* they were conceived in the order in which they were printed, I would point out that I am throughout concerned with the idea of arrangement itself as a second (or subsequent) stage of composition, and that individual poems of course take on additional meanings as they are ordered into a unified whole.

stantly bear in mind that at the time they wrote it was the latest minute in the history of the world, and they were as "modern" or "contemporary" as it was possible to be.) As everywhere in such "modern" Romantic poetry, the twofold problem is what attitude to take toward the loss and what action to pursue toward restoration. Although the sense of Keats's sestet is not crystal clear (the "leafy luxury" of pleasing Hunt with these poems is said to make up for the fact that "under pleasant trees / Pan is no longer sought"), the sonnet does suggest that lost glory and loveliness can be re-created, or at least compensated for, by poetry. "But there are left delights as high as these," delights of which "these poor offerings" are a sample.

The opening poem following the dedication, *I stood tip-toe*, is part description, part vision, part apostrophe, and has to do principally with the sources of poetic inspiration. After detailing his actual surroundings for a paragraph (1–28), Keats launches into a vision (29 ff.)—of nature, to be sure, but nature advanced from early spring ("sweet buds," "scantly leaved . . . stems" in ll. 3, 5) to the middle of summer (37)—that leads him eventually to an element of nature, the moon, which he apostrophizes as "Maker of sweet poets" (116). There are incidental references to poetry earlier (e.g., in ll. 50–52, on "great Apollo"), but it is only in the address to the moon (116–242) that Keats finally arrives at his main subject, the equation of nature with poetic inspiration: "For what has made the sage or poet write / But the fair paradise of Nature's light?" (125–126). That nature "Charms us at once away from all our troubles: / So that we feel uplifted from the world" (138–139) serves as an explanation of Keats's own visionary experience earlier in the poem, and also of the origins of the tales of Cupid and Psyche, Pan and Syrinx, Narcissus and Echo, and Endymion and Cynthia—this last the result of a vision in which the original poet "burst our mortal bars; / Into some wond'rous region he had gone" (190–191). In lines 193 ff. Keats briefly recounts the story of Endymion and Cynthia, describes several consequences of their union, and then breaks off with a question:

> Was there a Poet born?—but now no more,
> My wand'ring spirit must no further soar.— (241-242)

The question is ambiguous: Was there a poet conceived in the "greater blisses" (239) of the couple's wedding night? Was there a poet born in the original imagining of the tale? Was there a poet born *in Keats* in the telling of the story in *I stood tip-toe?* It can mean all these things, but especially the last. The connection between Keats's "wand'ring spirit . . . soar[ing]" in the final line and "burst[ing] our mortal bars" to search in "some wond'rous region" in lines 190–192 clinches the personal application of the question. In the over-all scheme of the volume, Keats is at this early point asking himself and his readers, in effect, "How am I doing so far?"[7]

In the next several poems Keats does not do so well. *Specimen of an Induction to a Poem* is the first of a number of pieces concerned with the chivalric past, nearer to the time when glory and loveliness had *not* passed away. The poet would "tell a tale of chivalry" (1, 11), "Revive the dying tones of minstrelsy" (32), give substance to his vision of white plumes, bright lance, and steed. But even a call for Spenser "to hover nigh / My daring steps" is unavailing, and neither this nor the fragmentary *Calidore* that it introduces comes to anything; the poet is obviously not yet ready to write the kind of poem he aspires to. The two poems in anapestic tetrameter composed for G. F. Mathew's sisters, *To Some Ladies* and *On Receiving a Curious Shell, and a Copy of Verses,* are of no importance except that the latter, in references to Armida, Rinaldo, Britomartis (8, 12), and a courteous knight named Eric (addressed throughout), continues the chivalric motifs of *Specimen* and *Calidore;* the reiterated statement that nature and poetry alike have "magical powers to bless, and to sooth" (20,

[7] Cf. "Muse of my native land, am I inspir'd?" in *Endymion,* IV.354.

44) echoes the same idea in *I stood tip-toe,* lines 138–139.[8] *To
* * * * (Mary Frogley) again looks back to "days of old" "when
chivalry / Lifted up her lance" (1, 41–42). *To Hope* has little
bearing on the over-all thematic concern with poetry, but it is
worth mentioning that one of the causes of despondency—"When
no fair dreams before my 'mind's eye' flit" (3)—is pretty clearly
the absence of *poetic* visions.[9] Any *Imitation of Spenser* is almost
by definition a poem about poetry; Keats's is one more instance of
personal longing to "Revive the dying tones of minstrelsy"—"Ah!
could I tell the wonders . . ." (19). Even in the sonnets (or, probably more accurately, sonnet-stanzas) [10] beginning "Woman!
when I behold thee," the speaker "hotly burn[s]—to be a Calidore— / A very Red Cross Knight . . . Might I be loved by thee
like these of yore" (12–14). I would not argue that these poems
were intentionally placed here as near failures, of course. But in
the over-all scheme of *Poems* they serve to show that a harking
back to days of yore, in an attempt to revive the old minstrelsy,
will not solve the problem posed by the dedicatory sonnet. Glory
and loveliness must be sought in something besides imitation of
the past.

[8] All told, there are seven passages in the volume bearing on the function
of poetry: *I stood tip-toe,* ll. 138–139; *On Receiving a Curious Shell,* ll.
19–20 (repeated in ll. 43–44); *Imitation of Spenser,* ll. 19–22; *To George
Felton Mathew,* ll. 63–65; *To My Brother George* (epistle), ll. 73–109;
Sleep and Poetry, ll. 245–247, 267–268. The Wordsworthian phrasing of
Sleep and Poetry, l. 247, "To sooth the cares, and lift the thoughts of man,"
pretty well epitomizes all the passages (cf. *Peter Bell,* l. 142, "To stir, to
soothe, or elevate").

[9] Cf. the failures of poetic vision in *To My Brother George* (epistle),
ll. 1–8, and the posthumously published sonnet *On Receiving a Laurel
Crown from Leigh Hunt.*

[10] In the format of the 1817 volume the three sonnets are clearly printed
as stanzas of a single poem. H. W. Garrod was right to number the lines
consecutively, 1–42, in his Oxford Standard Authors edition of *The Poetical
Works of John Keats* (London, 1956). In the line-numbering and editorial
apparatus of his Oxford English Texts edition, *The Poetical Works,* 2nd
ed. (Oxford, 1958), he treats the sonnet-stanzas as three separate poems.

Although the epigraph to the next section of poems, the Epistles, strikes an optimistic note—

> Among the rest a shepheard (though but young
> Yet hartned to his pipe) with all the skill
> His few yeeres could, began to fit his quill
> (Browne, *Britannia's Pastorals,* II.iii.748–750)

—the three epistles themselves disclose misgivings rather than hope. They have a buoyancy of tone befitting epistles actually sent (as these were) as letters, and contain the only intentionally humorous lines in the volume (e.g., the account of Mathew's "travels strange" in *To George Felton Mathew,* ll. 76–93, and the characterization of Clarke as a literary fondler of "maidens with the breasts of cream" in *To Charles Cowden Clarke,* ll. 33–34). But instead of "heartening" and "fitting," Keats tells of impediments to writing and doubts about his ability. In the epistle to Mathew, generally celebrating the pleasures of verse and "a brotherhood in song" (1–2), the prospect for Keats is all too gloomy: though he would "fain . . . follow thee [Mathew] / Past each horizon of fine poesy" (11–12), his medical studies stand in the way—

> far different cares
> Beckon me sternly from soft "Lydian airs,"
> And hold my faculties so long in thrall,
> That I am oft in doubt whether at all
> I shall again see Phœbus. . . .   (17–21)

But even had he unlimited time to give to his coy muse, "with me she would not live / In this dark city" (31–33). The epistle *To My Brother George,* which comes just at the middle of the volume, deals in order with inspiration and the poetic process (1–66, again with a glance back at "time of old" in ll. 17–18); fame— "posterity's award"—and the good influence of poetry (67–109); and then the question of Keats's personal aims (109 ff.). The conclusion Keats reaches here, before going on to the quiet description of seaside surroundings with which the poem closes, is that his desire for poetic fame is a "mad ambition," and that he would be "Happier, and dearer to society" by forsaking it, presumably in favor of some more practically useful career like medicine. The epistle to Clarke is the most relaxed of the three, but, even so, Keats is only half joking when he declares himself to be as poetically ineffectual as a swan trying to keep drops of water from running off his wing:

> Just like that bird am I in loss of time,
> Whene'er I venture on the stream of rhyme;
> With shatter'd boat, oar snapt, and canvass rent,
> I slowly sail, scarce knowing my intent. . . .   (15-18)

Perhaps Keats is being overly ambitious.[11] At any rate, the youthful shepherd, having "fit his quill," now pipes on simpler subjects and with a considerable reduction of scope in the next section of poems, the Sonnets. Almost all of the sonnets are about *pleasures*—nature, poetry, roses, women, the fireside at home, conversation, the discovery of Homer, and so on—and in this sense they may be thought of as brief explorations into the subject-matter for poetry. But nine of the seventeen poems have some specific bearing on the thematic concern with poetry that dominates the volume. *Written on the Day that Mr. Leigh Hunt Left Prison* describes the poetic imagination in operation ("To regions of his own his genius true / Took happy flights"); *How many bards* pronounces on the good influence of past poets; *To My Brothers* contains incidental references to the search for rhymes and to "poetic sleep"; *Keen, fitful gusts* echoes the epistles in celebrating the combined pleasures of friendship and poetry; *On*

---

[11] After the epistle to Clarke, Keats next uses navigation metaphors in this way when he is thinking about the "long Poem" that became *Endymion*: "a long Poem is a test of Invention which I take to be the Polar Star of Poetry, as Fancy is the Sails, and Imagination the Rudder" (from a lost letter to George, spring 1817, which Keats extracts in a letter to Benjamin Bailey of 8 October 1817—*The Letters of John Keats*, ed. Hyder E. Rollins, Cambridge, Mass., 1958, I, 170).

First Looking into Chapman's Homer records the excitement Keats felt on discovering a new realm of poetry; *On Leaving Some Friends at an Early Hour* fairly bursts with eagerness to "write down a line of glorious tone"; the two sonnets addressed to Haydon discourse on fame and genius (two of the three identifiable "Great spirits" are poets); *On the Grasshopper and Cricket* again links nature and poetry in the concept of "The poetry of earth." There is no progression in theme or quality within the sonnets; but, unlike the earlier fragments, each is a complete poem, and as a group they are generally better (in some instances, as *Keen, fitful gusts,* the Chapman's Homer sonnet, and *On the Grasshopper and Cricket,* markedly better) than any of the pieces between *I stood tip-toe* and the epistles. They were, of course, in most cases written more recently; but a part of their superiority must be attributed to Keats's abandonment of "days of old" in favor of subjects and experiences more immediate to his senses. The sonnets repeatedly emphasize the present: "Many the wonders I *this day* have seen"; "Small, busy flames *play . . .*"; "Keen, fitful gusts *are* whisp'ring . . ."; "Great spirits *now* on earth . . ."; "The poetry of earth *is never* dead"; "Happy *is* England!" And they contain social sentiments ("the social thought of thee," "friendliness unquell'd," "two kindred spirits," "brimful of . . . friendliness") that have no counterpart in the earlier poems preceding the epistles. In the over-all structure of the volume, the sonnets stand as sufficient cause for the renewal of optimism that appears in the final poem, *Sleep and Poetry.*

There are more difficult interpretive problems in *Sleep and Poetry* than in any of the other early poems (problems concerning the connection between sleep and poetry; the role of the charioteer in ll. 125–154, and the source of what he writes down in ll. 151–154; the seeming confusion of pronouns in ll. 154, 165, 167; and so on). But there is no ambiguity about the firmness of Keats's self-dedication to poetry in this poem. *Sleep and Poetry* is both a justification of much of the verse in his first volume and

a program for development to more significant achievement in
the future. The apostrophe to Poesy in lines 47–84 begins with the
same leafy "luxury" and "fair / Visions of . . . bowery nook"
and other woodsy places that were the main stuff of the earlier
poems (cf. "bowery clefts" and "tasteful nook" in *I stood tip-toe*, ll.
21, 30, "flowery spot" in the epistle to Mathew, l. 37, and "leafy
nook" in the epistle to Clark, l. 36); it concludes, however, with a
promise to seize "the events of this wide world . . . Like a strong
giant." This progress from escapist elysian bowers to the more
pressing concerns of *this* world is reiterated, after a paragraph on
the brevity of human life, in the famous passage that begins,

> O for ten years, that I may overwhelm
> Myself in poesy; so I may do the deed
> That my own soul has to itself decreed.   (96 ff.)

"First the realm I'll pass / Of Flora, and old Pan" (101–102)—the
realm, that is, of *Poems* of 1817 (with perhaps a glance toward
Endymion, which Keats would begin a month after the volume
was published). Then the poet will embark on "a nobler life, /
Where I may find the agonies, the strife / Of human hearts"
(123–125). (On sitting down to reread *King Lear* at the beginning of 1818, Keats would bid farewell to romance; the best
poems of 1818 and especially those of 1819 centrally concern "the
agonies, the strife / Of human hearts.") There are "doubtings,"
just as in the epistle *To My Brother George,* but also a heretofore
undeclared resolve to overcome them (159–160). Having seen
"The end and aim of Poesy" (245–247, 267–268, 292–293), and
with a "vast idea" ever rolling before him—the idea is not defined, but surely it has to do with poetic fame—Keats brushes
aside further misgivings about his abilities. Even if he is madman
or Icarus, he has set himself a task, and to "unsay" those resolu-
tions is "impossible! / Impossible!" (310–312). To the question
at the end of *I stood tip-toe*—"Was there a Poet born?"—the
final poem of the volume provides a convincing affirmative: there

was a poet born, these are his first productions, and there's more
—and better—to come.

In summary: the pieces that make up *Poems* of 1817 can, almost without exception, be seen as dealing with the question of
Keats's career as a poet.[12] A problem is stated in the dedicatory
sonnet—"Glory and loveliness have passed away"—and it is
hinted that a solution may lie in the pleasures and power of
poetry. *I stood tip-toe,* treating poetic inspiration and bringing
the problem around to Keats personally with the question "Was
there a Poet born?" is followed by a series of fragmentary and
imitative attempts to re-create lost glory and loveliness, testing
as it were the suggestion of the dedicatory sonnet. Not surpris-
ingly, the feebleness of these early compositions raises doubts in
Keats's mind about his qualifications to be a poet, and the epistles
that come next searchingly consider the question of whether he
should continue his efforts or give poetry over for some more
active and socially useful career. With the sonnets, Keats seems
to begin anew, and on a smaller scale. In these he is more successful, and so with fresh enthusiasm in the final poem of the
volume he dedicates himself firmly to a life of poetry, and lays
down a ten-year program in which he will progress from visions
of leafy luxury to a more serious confrontation of human problems and the events of this wide world. At least for this earliest
volume, *Sleep and Poetry* decisively settles the question of Keats's
career as a poet, and points the way not only toward restoring
glory and loveliness but toward easing the pain—soothing the
cares, and lifting the thoughts—of man. *Endymion* and the poems
of 1818 and 1819 proceed from there.

[12] A few of the early poems and about half of the sonnets (*To Some
Ladies, To Hope, Woman! when I behold thee,* Sonnets I, II, V–VIII, X,
XVI, XVII) do not bear in any very direct way on the topic. I think it is
probably for just this reason that Keats included the apologetic note quoted
above in n. 5, though at least three of the sonnets listed here were written
after the summer of 1816.

✑ On the Interpretation of *Endymion:* The Comedian as the Letter E

In 1940, well before the Wallace Stevens critical industry got under way, Hi Simons began an essay on *The Comedian as the Letter C* with the observation, "Since it was brought out in *Harmonium,* in 1923, eight theories for its interpretation have been proposed. But these hypotheses are mutually contradictory. . . . So their net effect is to cancel each other out."[1] This is not quite the situation with criticism of *Endymion,* but there have been many interpretations—well over a hundred since F. M. Owen's *John Keats: A Study* appeared in 1880, and some thirty of them of major proportions. While it can hardly be said that they are all "mutually contradictory" or that they cancel one another out, they do in many ways conflict, and none has been found (except perhaps by its author) wholly satisfactory as a comprehensive explanation of Keats's intentions in the poem.[2] My purpose here

---

[1] "'The Comedian as the Letter C': Its Sense and Its Significance," *Southern Review,* V (1940), 453–468 (reprinted in *The Achievement of Wallace Stevens,* ed. Ashley Brown and Robert S. Haller, Philadelphia and New York, 1962, pp. 97–113).

[2] Among criticism of the last two decades I would cite Jacob D. Wigod, "The Meaning of *Endymion,*" *PMLA,* LXVIII (1953), 779–790; Glen O. Allen, "The Fall of Endymion: A Study in Keats's Intellectual Growth," *Keats-Shelley Journal,* VI (1957), 37–57; Carroll Arnett, "Thematic Structure in Keats's *Endymion,*" *Texas Studies in English,* XXXVI (1957), 100–109; Clarisse Godfrey, *"Endymion,"* in *John Keats: A Reassessment,* ed. Kenneth Muir (Liverpool, 1958), pp. 20–38; Albert Gérard, "Keats and the Romantic *Sehnsucht,*" *University of Toronto Quarterly,* XXVIII (1959), 160–175 (reprinted in Gérard's *English Romantic Poetry,* Berkeley and Los

is not to arbitrate among the principal interpretations, or even to offer one of my own, but rather—much less ambitiously—to attempt to explain why there have been so many.

I

My main point, if I may set it down at the beginning rather than at the end, is that there are a number of central themes running through Keats's poem. Interpretations have dealt with one or more of these, sometimes with several, but not, at once, with all of them. I shall single out five for brief discussion, giving partial documentation of the relevant passages in quasi-tabular form.

(1) *"Fellowship with essence"—a kind of imaginative joining or identification with things and persons outside oneself that leads, at its highest reach, to union with some ideal.* Many critics before, and all critics after, Newell F. Ford [3] have been aware of this theme, which not only is the subject of an impressive speech by

Angeles, 1968, pp. 194-214); Stuart M. Sperry, Jr., "The Allegory of *Endymion,*" *Studies in Romanticism,* II (1962), 38-53; Walter H. Evert, *Aesthetic and Myth in the Poetry of Keats* (Princeton, 1965), pp. 88-176; Bruce E. Miller, "On the Meaning of Keats's *Endymion,*" *Keats-Shelley Journal,* XIV (1965), 33-54; Mario L. D'Avanzo, "Keats's and Vergil's Underworlds: Source and Meaning in Book II of *Endymion,*" *Keats-Shelley Journal,* XVI (1967), 61-72; Helen E. Haworth, "The Redemption of Cynthia," *Humanities Association Bulletin,* XVIII (1967), 80-91; Northrop Frye, *"Endymion:* The Romantic Epiphanic," *A Study of English Romanticism* (New York, 1968), pp. 125-165. For surveys of the views of important earlier critics—among them Robert Bridges, Ernest de Selincourt, Sidney Colvin, Amy Lowell, Clarence D. Thorpe, J. M. Murry, Leonard Brown, Douglas Bush, C. L. Finney, and Newell F. Ford—see in particular the articles by Wigod, Sperry, and Miller. Evert, pp. 115-118, has a fine note illustrating some of the "inconsistencies and contradictions with which the interpreter of the poem must contend." I have assumed from the outset that the question of whether or not the poem is allegorical is no longer an issue, and that the main problem is (once again) the interpretation of the allegory.

[3] See especially his "The Meaning of 'Fellowship with Essence' in *Endymion,*" *PMLA,* LXII (1947), 1061-76.

Endymion (I.777 ff.) [4] and is easily seen as one description of
Endymion's quest throughout the poem, but also is a concept im-
bedded in much of the incidental language—in the verbs "bind,"
"commune," "melt into," "blend," "mingle," "interknit," "com-
bine," "commingle," for example. It is obviously related to Keats's
notion of Negative Capability, though the letters most frequently
cited for that idea (27[?] December 1817 and 27 October 1818,
Letters, I, 193–194, 386–387) were written after the first draft of
the poem was completed, and the earlier of them seems to speak
of it as a recent discovery ("several things dovetailed in my mind,
& at once it struck me . . ."). Among passages relevant to this
theme are the following:

I.30–31, 36–37 (two brief instances of identification with "essence");
　98–100 ("melt out . . . essence . . . Into the winds"); 540–678
　(Endymion's dream-union with Cynthia—see especially ll. 594–595,
　600); 777–849 (the full-scale explanation—note the language of ll.
　784–785, 796, 798–799, 810–813, 833); 902 ("Bathing my spirit").
II.12 ("in our very souls, we feel"); 274–284 (self and solitude, the op-
　posites of "fellowship"); 707–827 (another dream-union with the
　goddess—note ll. 739–740, 752, 815–817); 835–839 (poet's immer-
　sion in a "sleeping lake").
III.55 ("thine airy fellowship"); 162–173 (the moon's blending with
　Endymion's "ardours"); 380–391 (Glaucus' self-destroying entan-
　glement with the ocean); 766 ff. (the "mighty consummation" of
　Glaucus and Scylla and the other lovers); 963 ("blend and inter-
　knit").
IV.92 ff. (Endymion's love for the Indian maiden); 477 ("no self-pas-
　sion or identity"); 512–551 (the Cave of Quietude); 977–1002 (the
　final union with Cynthia).

---

　[4] A speech perhaps made more impressive by Keats's assurance to his
publisher John Taylor, 30 January 1818, "that when I wrote it, it was a
regular stepping of the Imagination towards a Truth. My having written
that Argument will perhaps be of the greatest Service to me of any thing
I ever did" (*The Letters of John Keats,* ed. Hyder E. Rollins, Cambridge,
Mass., 1958, I, 218).

(2) *"Gradations of Happiness"* [5]—*the idea of a valuation scale of "essences."* This, again based on Endymion's speech in I.777 ff., is clearly subordinate to, or a part of, the preceding motif. But it has been treated separately in so many critical discussions that it has acquired independent status as a theme of the poem. The principal passages are the following:

I.540 ff. (Endymion's dream experiences begin with nature and the moon, and end with the goddess); 777 ff. (progression from rose leaf and music to friendship, mortal love, and immortal love).

In Book II there is a progression of sorts from solitude to concern for nature (from which Endymion is separated) and then love (the Venus and Adonis episode and the second dream-union with Cynthia).

III.23–40 (describing a "ladder" to heavenly "regalities"); [6] 142–179 (Endymion's retrospective account of his relationship with the moon—again a progression beginning with nature and going on to higher fellowship).

IV.851–854 (distinction between "pleasures real" and "higher ones"). At the end of Book IV Endymion achieves the highest fellowship on the scale.

(3) *The conflict of self and solitude with love and humanitarian activities.* This would be at least partly subsumable under (1), the theme of "fellowship," were it not that at certain points in the poem human and divine relationships are directly opposed to one another. In any case, because of the peculiar connection between Keats's poem and Shelley's *Alastor* (see section II, below), which prominently treats solitude and self-love, the theme must be listed

---

[5] In the same letter to Taylor (see n. 4) Keats goes on to say that Endymion's speech in Book I "set before me at once the gradations of Happiness even like a kind of Pleasure Thermometer."

[6] It should be noted, however, that these lines are philosophically quite unspecific. Though a ladder is mentioned in l. 26, there is otherwise no suggestion of gradations or scales—simply the assertion that "A thousand Powers" exist, largely unseen except as they are represented in clouds and other elements of the sky. The passage is an introduction to Keats's eulogy of the moon.

separately. In his quest for union with Cynthia, Endymion renounces the world and worldly activities; in much of the poem
he is a "solitary." A sizable group of critics,[7] pointing to Endymion's actions in sympathizing with Alpheus and Arethusa in
Book II, freeing the drowned lovers in Book III, and pitying and
falling in love with the (seemingly) mortal Indian maiden in
Book IV, take it as Keats's main point that Endymion must be
schooled in the ways of *human* existence before he can gain immortality. The following may be cited:

I.721 ff. (the whole exchange between Peona and Endymion, especially
  the conflict of earthly fame and "high and noble life"—ostensibly
  the performance of humanitarian deeds—with love, as in ll. 757–
  760 and 816–842).

II.77–78 (Endymion in "a solitary glen, / Where there was never sound
  of mortal men": he is separated from the human world for all of
  Books II and III and much of Book IV); 274–293 ("habitual self,"
  the "deadly feel of solitude"); 586–587, 590, 633, 681–682, 706, 857–
  860 (six references to solitude and loneliness); 1012–17 (Endymion's sympathy for Alpheus and Arethusa, and prayer to Cynthia to aid them).[8]

III.282–290 (Endymion's heart "warm[s] / With pity"); 386 (Glaucus'
  "Forgetful utterly of self-intent" again relates anti-self to "fellowship," the idea of "self-destroying" enthrallments in I.798–799);

---

[7] Douglas Bush's writings, from *Mythology and the Romantic Tradition
in English Poetry* (Cambridge, Mass., 1937) through *John Keats: His Life
and Writings* (New York and London, 1966), have been notably influ-
ential. The fullest explications in terms of "spiritualization-through-human-
ization" are those by Wigod and Evert. It is probably fair to say that,
among more recent discussions, this is the majority view of the principal
meaning of Keats's allegory.

[8] The point of the Alpheus-Arethusa incident may indeed be Endymion's
awakening humanitarianism. But much more is made of the fact that it is
Cynthia and Arethusa's vow of chastity to her that cause the trouble between the lovers, at a time when Cynthia herself secretly burns for Endymion, with whom (in a dream) she has just made love. The irony is
emphasized in Endymion's addressing his prayer to the unknown "Goddess of my pilgrimage," who is, of course, Cynthia.

714 ff. (Endymion's "achievement high" in freeing the lovers, for which he is apparently rewarded—see ll. 1023-24).

IV.475-477 ("no self-passion or identity"). Book IV is largely concerned with love, and especially with Endymion's human feelings (pity, love, perplexity) in relation to the Indian maiden.

(4) *The opposing claims of human and immortal realms of existence.* This is partly related to the preceding concern, and involves some of the same passages cited for it, but is primarily a metaphysical or "ontological" [9] rather than a social or moral theme. Endymion's rhetorical question of I.777 asks, among other things, whether happiness lies in the actual world or in some ideal realm, [10] and through much of his quest he is intent on freeing himself from the one in order to gain entrance to the other. This motif especially shows up in incidental details of the poem, as in the first three instances below:

I.7 ("bind us to the earth"); 68-72 (the lamb straying out of the actual world); 176-177 ("like one who dream'd / Of . . . groves Elysian"); 360-393 (the old shepherds' ideas of heaven—note the tone of "wander'd," "vieing to rehearse," "fond imaginations" in ll. 371, 372, 393); 404 ("Like one who on the earth had never stept"); 473-474 ("Can I want . . . aught nearer heaven"); 505-507 (Endymion knows of "things . . . Immortal, starry"); 621-622, 681-705 (immortal dream vs. reality); 721 ff. (again, Peona's speech on the claims of this world, and Endymion's reply justifying his longing for the higher realm); 972-977 (Endymion's temporary resolution "to fashion / My pilgrimage for the world's dusky brink"—and not beyond).

II.123-125 (the idea of wandering "far . . . past the scanty bar / To mortal steps"); 142-162 (Endymion's analogy for human life,

[9] See Miller's essay, cited in n. 2.

[10] In "Imagination and Reality in the Odes," below, I provide a simple diagram of the two realms and a collection of terms commonly applied to them. This "ontological" theme, like that concerning the authenticity of dreams (see the next paragraph), is of course particularly relevant to Keats's later poems.

which he rejects); 185–187 (more bursting of mortal bars); 302–332 (Endymion's plea, as "exil'd mortal," for deliverance "from this rapacious deep"); 463–464 (Adonis failed to seize "heaven"); 904–909 ("earthly root . . . bloom of heaven").

III.374–378 (Glaucus' "distemper'd longings" for another world); 906–907 (the idea of escape "from dull mortality's harsh net"); 1007 ("far strayed from mortality"); 1024–27 ("Immortal bliss . . . endless heaven").

IV.36–37 (the Indian maiden's plea for "one short hour / Of native air"); 298–320, 614–723, 851–854 (Endymion's internal conflict in these passages and throughout much of Book IV over the choice between the Indian maiden and his goddess). At the end of Book IV, when the Indian maiden reveals herself as Cynthia, Endymion in a sense wins both worlds.

(5) *The authenticity of dreams, which here (as in a number of Keats's later poems) are meant to symbolize the visionary imagination.* The invitation to make much of this theme and a guarantee of the symbolism of dreaming in the poem are seemingly offered by Keats himself in the letter to Benjamin Bailey of 22 November 1817 in which he states his certainty in "the authenticity of the Imagination": "you may know my favorite Speculation by my first Book" (of *Endymion,* presumably referring especially to Peona's questioning of dreams—"how light / Must dreams themselves be. . . . Why pierce high-fronted honour to the quick / For nothing but a dream?"—and Endymion's reply urging the reality of his dream experience). "What the imagination seizes as Beauty must be truth," Keats says, and he goes on to compare imagination to Adam's dream in Book VIII of *Paradise Lost:* "he awoke and found it truth" (*Letters,* I, 184–185). Critics [11] have seen Endymion's quest as a testing of the authenticity of dreams, and there is, most prominently in Books I and IV, a good deal of evidence to support the idea:

[11] Most notably Allen and Sperry, in the articles cited in n. 2, and Earl R. Wasserman, *The Finer Tone: Keats' Major Poems* (Baltimore, 1953), especially the chapter on *The Eve of St. Agnes.*

I.22-24 (tales as "immortal drink" from "heaven's brink"); 176-177 (Endymion's seeming to dream of Elysium is an early clue); 288-289, 293-302 (Pan as a symbol of imagination, giving "clodded earth . . . a touch ethereal"); 324-325 (history sending "A young mind from its bodily tenement"); 360-393 (again, the old shepherds' "fond imaginations," which, while not dreams, are nevertheless types of visionary experience); 455-463 (sleep, dreams, visionary "enchantment"); 540-678 (Endymion's dream experiences—note ll. 573-578, 581-586); 717-722, 747-760 (Peona's remarks on Endymion's "weakness" and the lightness of dreams—"whims," "mere nothing"); 769 ff. (Endymion's reply—see especially ll. 770-771, 850-861).

II.43 (Endymion is said to be "Brain-sick"—cf. I.758); 437-439 (the presentation of "immortal bowers to mortal sense"); 703-708 (dreaming as an escape from solitude).

III.440-443, 460, 476 (Glaucus' "love dream" is a "specious heaven").

IV.407-436 (Endymion dreams of heaven and his goddess, and then "Beheld awake his very dream"); 636-659, 669 (Endymion's renunciation of dreams [12]—in a passage, however, described as "fancies vain and crude," 722, the product of his desperation and frustration). At the end of the poem Endymion's dream turns out—as since Book II we knew it would—to be a "truth."

There are other preoccupations in the poem—one might include (6) "the playing of different Natures with Joy and Sorrow" (*Letters,* I, 219—for the *Endymion* references see "joy," "grief," "sorrow" in the Keats concordance); (7) Keats's curious emphasis here and there on *midwayness* (see "bourne," "brink," "half," "middle," "midway" in the concordance, and the mention of "a space of life between" in the fourth paragraph of the Preface to *Endymion*); and (8) the extent to which Endymion is, as Keats wrote in two letters of 23 January 1818, "led on . . . by circumstance" and "overshadowed by a Supernatural Power" (*Letters,* I, 207, 213—in the poem see II.123-128, 293, 574-575; III.297-

---

[12] It is worth noting that Keats wrote these lines only a few days after his 22 November 1817 letter to Bailey.

299, 708, 759, 1023; IV.976, 990). Still other topics could be added to the list. But the first five items I have set out briefly above are, I think, the main themes of the poem.

Now comes the knotty problem of relationships among them. All five of the themes appear in the dialogue between Peona and Endymion in the last half of Book I, and there are obvious connections made (or to be made) among them: the idea of gradations (2) is embodied in the exposition of "fellowship with essence" (1); self and solitude (3) are opposed to "fellowship" (1), while love and humanity (3) are high on the scale; both the human and the divine realms (4) are areas in which love and, in a sense, humanity (3) are possible; dreams (5) are posited as a means to highest fellowship (1), which is a type of immortal existence (4); and so on. On the other hand, certain oppositions may be observed: dreaming (5) is antithetical to human love and humanitarian deeds (3), and these—and the whole human realm (4)—are renounced for higher fellowship (1); dreaming (5) also may ultimately be opposed to highest fellowship (1)—in the commonest critical reading of the poem it is necessary for Endymion to repudiate his ideal in order to win it. All five themes have to be considered in any comprehensive interpretation of the poem, and, as I suggested at the outset, the critics, while dealing with one or more of them, or even with partial elements of all of them, have not managed to reconcile them in a single, unified explanation of the poem. There is good reason for this.

All five of the themes are, loosely speaking, "philosophical," but they do not all belong to the same branch of philosophy. In varying degrees they have implications that are social (1-4), moral (1, 3, 4), metaphysical (1, 2, 4, 5), psychological (1, 3, 5), and aesthetic (1, 2, 5), but there is no one category in which all five can be related into a consistency. In particular, owing to Keats's peculiar emphases in the poem, there is a point at which the social-moral concerns on the one hand (very roughly, 1-4) and the psychological-aesthetic concerns on the other (taking for the moment 5 by itself) [13] do not seem to impinge on one another. It is not so much that they conflict as that they simply have nothing to do with one another. The difficulty may, of course, be merely our own (or my own) critical shortsightedness, but I prefer to offer another explanation.

II

I think a clarification, though not a resolution, of the problem can be found in Shelley's *Alastor* (published in March 1816, thirteen months before Keats began his poem), which has long been recognized as a precipitating element in *Endymion*.[14] It is, of course, possible to read *Alastor* in a number of different ways. Two of these are more relevant than the others to the question at hand, and I shall outline them briefly.[15] (1) *Alastor* is, among other things, an allegorical representation of an unfortunate state of

[13] If the question of authenticity of dreams (5) is thus isolatable from the others, it might be thought the easiest solution to the problem simply to drop the theme from the list. But its importance to Keats in several hundred lines of Books I and IV, especially in view of the fervor with which Endymion defends the idea at the beginning of his wanderings and attempts to renounce it near the end, cannot be denied.

[14] See Leonard Brown, "The Genesis, Growth, and Meaning of *Endymion*," *Studies in Philology*, XXX (1933), 618–653. There are enough similarities and echoes of narrative and descriptive detail in *Endymion* as to leave no doubt that Keats had *Alastor* in mind while writing his poem.

[15] I am aware that in dealing with *Alastor* I have at hand another of those Romantic poems (there is a distinguished group of them that includes *Tintern Abbey*, the *Intimations* ode, *The Rime of the Ancient Mariner*, *Kubla Khan*, and several of Keats's odes) that have not been definitively interpreted and on which there is an immense body of critical literature. Here, however, I am not so much concerned with what Shelley may have intended in the poem (in any event, the Preface and the poem do not cohere, and the second paragraph of the Preface has seemingly unresolvable internal inconsistencies) as with two meanings that I think, on the evidence of *Endymion*, Keats himself was most conscious of. If the interpretations depend more than they should on Shelley's Preface, it ought to be remembered that Keats read that Preface, and without benefit of the critical explications of the last four decades.

mind and the effects that follow from it. The state of mind is self-love; the effects are loss of sympathy or response in nature, physical wasting away, and ultimately death. Shelley's Poet goes happily about seeking and gathering knowledge until the need for love suddenly and necessarily awakens in him, and he has a vision. This vision, combining the attraction of a beloved woman with certain attributes of nature, is the creation of the Poet's imagination, and it comes near being an idealization of the Poet's self, his own soul, stripped of all imperfections (Shelley's fragmentary essay "On Love" is frequently cited in connection with this aspect of the vision; see also the first paragraph of Shelley's Preface to *Alastor* and ll. 153–161 of the poem). In the course of his long search, for a human embodiment of this vision or reunion with the prototype, the Poet's quest gradually turns into one of yearning after self (and hence the Poet's rejection of humanity and his increasing involvement in solitude, the "self-centred seclusion" of Shelley's Preface). If there is an *alastor* in the poem, it is the Poet's self-love. He wastes away and dies at the end principally because he has, in seeking after his love-vision, become enamored of himself (the narcissuses in ll. 406–408 are one of several clues), and because he has excluded "sweet human love" (see especially ll. 60–63, 129–139, 203–205, 266–271).

(2) *Alastor* may also be read as an exposition of an epistemological dilemma involving imagination, creativity, and association psychology. Here the question would be how, if (in the theories of Locke and Hartley) dreams and visions are no more than simple and complex recollections of sense experience, can any new truths outside the material world be apprehended?—or, to put it in Keats's terms, how can the imagination be "authentic"? *Alastor* has clearly an associationist bias—note "sinks . . . into the frame of his conceptions," "modifications," "intellectual faculties, the imagination, the functions of sense," "attaching . . . to a single image" in the first paragraph of the Preface, and "vacant mind" in line 126. Shelley's Poet takes in impressions until his mind is

saturated, and he has exhausted the natural world. He then, in quest of novelty, creates a love-vision which, because it is actually based on his own past sensations, is too much like his knowledge of himself. He seeks in vain for a prototype that in reality has no existence outside himself, and then dies, "Blasted by his disappointment." In this reading,[16] *Alastor* is a denial of the imagination's ability to provide authentic transcendental truths—"What the imagination seizes as Beauty" proves to be a false lure—and the poem is a calmly despairing lament over the situation.

We have here, then, two thematic preoccupations in Shelley's poem that, while they are not incompatible, are not really relatable any more than the social-moral and psychological-aesthetic themes of *Endymion*. It is primarily these two concerns that I think Keats responded to in his own poem. To the one he provided a positive answer. Where the Poet in *Alastor* had renounced the world, spurned human love, pursued a vision of idealized self, failed in his quest, and died, Endymion, beginning on the same course, learns sympathy, performs humanitarian deeds, experiences human love, and finally succeeds, being rewarded with "Immortal bliss." In the other matter Keats is less conclusive. Although Endymion's love-dream does turn out to be a truth, as the *Alastor*-Poet's did not, Endymion seemingly has serious misgivings toward the end of the poem—

> I have clung
> To nothing, lov'd a nothing, nothing seen
> Or felt but a great dream! O I have been
> Presumptuous against love, against the sky,
> Against all elements, against the tie
> Of mortals each to each. . . .
>   . . . so my story

[16] Among critical studies of the poem, the interpretation closest to the one offered in this paragraph is that by Albert Gérard, *"Alastor,* or the Spirit of Solipsism," *Philological Quarterly,* XXXIII (1954), 164-177 (reprinted in revised form in Gérard's *English Romantic Poetry,* pp. 136-162).

Will I to children utter, and repent.
There never liv'd a mortal man, who bent
His appetite beyond his natural sphere,
But starv'd and died. . . .
                              . . . gone and past
Are cloudy phantasms. Caverns lone, farewel!
And air of visions, and the monstrous swell
Of visionary seas! No, never more
Shall airy voices cheat me . . .   (IV.636–654)

—and there is good reason, especially in the light of his later
poems, to think that Keats shared them, in spite of the happy
ending he wrote into his poem. My point, however, is not here to
argue for Keats's skepticism concerning the visionary imagination,
but rather to show how an unrelatedness of themes in *Endymion*
is paralleled in a similar unrelatedness of themes in *Alastor,*
known to be one of the sources of Keats's poem. If we are assign-
ing blame for faulty unity, then part of it must fall on Shelley.

III

I do not, however, think blame is called for, and I would maintain that such thematic unrelatednesses are quite common in long
poems. I began this essay, and chose my title, in anticipation of
making a concluding point using parallels in a more modern
allegory. Though Wallace Stevens read *Endymion* at least twice,
in 1899 and 1909,[17] one would hardly call it an immediate stimulus
to *The Comedian as the Letter C,* which was written in the early
1920's. Yet Stevens' poem does in some ways begin where *Endymion* leaves off, and it vaguely bears something of the same
thematic relationship to Keats's poem as *Endymion* bears to
Alastor.

[17] *Letters of Wallace Stevens,* ed. Holly Stevens (New York, 1966), pp.
28–29, 147–148. He also saw Keats's fair copy of the poem, now in the
Pierpont Morgan Library, in 1908 (p. 110).

In Part I, "The World without Imagination," Stevens' Crispin (who is both a poet in search of an aesthetic and a pilgrim-wanderer in search of an inhabitable world) is on the first leg of a voyage from "Bordeaux to Yucatan, Havana next, / And then to Carolina" (54–55). At sea, tempest-tossed and overwhelmed by the immensity of the ocean, he is reduced to "some starker, barer self / In a starker, barer world" (61–62): "The last distortion of romance / Forsook the insatiable egotist" (76–77). In Yucatan (Part II) Crispin, arriving "destitute" (96), engorges himself on "savage color" (103) and "Green barbarism" (125), finding "A new reality in parrot-squawks" (148). Part III plays off "moonlight" yearnings against "the essential prose" of realistic detail. Crispin's journey is "A fluctuating between sun and moon" (234), and as he approaches Carolina "The moonlight fiction disappeared" (257): "He gripped more closely the essential prose / As being, in a world so falsified, / The one integrity for him" (274–276). In Part IV Crispin projects a colony on the premises of the value of essential prose. Romance is banished ("Exit the mental moonlight," 284), and fiction and dreams as well ("All dreams are vexing. Let them be expunged," 377); the sole value is "veracious page on page, exact" (381). In Part V Crispin, further reducing his scope "To things within his actual eye" (394), builds a cabin, marries, and settles down to "what is" (438)—a "quotidian" that, if it saps philosophers (460), nevertheless consists of food, birds, flowers, and lovemaking. Part VI, which introduces his four daughters, shows the hero now leading the same kind of life he led in Bordeaux. The realization of the circularity of his pilgrimage engenders a fatalistic skepticism, which produces the "doctrine" of lines 540 ff.:

> Crispin concocted doctrine from the rout.
> The world, a turnip once so readily plucked,
> Sacked up and carried overseas, daubed out
> Of its ancient purple, pruned to the fertile main,

> And sown again by the stiffest realist,
> Came reproduced in purple, family font,
> The same insoluble lump.

The lines, which may be read as retracing the "action" of the poem, conclude with the idea that Crispin's new world is "The same insoluble lump" with which he began.

I suppose the general drift of the story is clear enough: Crispin the romantic settles down as Crispin the realist. But there are a number of things that stand in the way of more detailed interpretation. The progress from section to section is sometimes confusing—for example, the shifts from romanticism to bare realism to "exotic realism" and then back to bare realism in Parts I–III seem arbitrary rather than reasonably motivated. And one is left in doubt about the attitude of the poem toward Crispin's situation in the final section: is it supposed to be an arrival or a falling-off? A special difficulty, which may relate the poem more immediately to the present discussion of *Endymion* and *Alastor,* is the introduction of a social theme. "Mythology of self" and "insatiable egotist" at the outset (20, 77) have primarily an epistemological reference, and are related to an initial theory of imagination in lines 1–2 ("man is the intelligence of his soil, / The sovereign ghost") that is subsequently discarded for that at the opening of Part IV ("his soil is man's intelligence. / That's better. That's worth crossing seas to find," 280–281). So too with "the relentless contact he desired" (215) and "The liaison, the blissful liaison, / Between himself and his environment" in Part III, even though this liaison is said to be "chief motive, first delight . . . *and not for him alone*" (221–224, italics mine). But at least beginning in Part V, if not earlier in the notion of colonizing, social considerations appear in the poem: Part V opens with "Crispin as hermit" (382), and in the next 150 lines he enters into marriage and the rearing of a family. And though the marriage serves in part to build up the picture of the "quotidian," and the four daughters are almost certainly symbolic (they are "Four questioners and four sure answerers," 539, which may, however, strike some fathers as a believable description of real daughters), still they involve Crispin in social ties that he has earlier been conspicuously free from. Line 489, "The return to social nature," is an additional clue.[18] Other critics besides Hi Simons have discovered social preoccupations in the poem, and others besides him have foundered in interpreting Parts V and VI. Some of the difficulty may be the same that I have set forth to explain why critics have written incompletely about *Endymion:* the social-moral and psychological-aesthetic concerns do not always cohere.

Stevens declared in 1935, in connection with *The Comedian,* that he had "the greatest dislike for explanations. As soon as people are perfectly sure of a poem they are just as likely as not to have no further interest in it; it loses whatever potency it had." [19] I do not agree, but there is a risk, in the kind of monothematic explanation that Stevens probably had in mind, of oversimplifying and distorting the works we seek to clarify. For some reason not clear to me, in dealing with a "difficult" modern like Stevens the critics tend to accept what they cannot work into their systems, while in dealing with earlier poets like Keats and Shelley they more often take a condescending view, blaming the poets for the immaturity of their conceptions. It is more reasonable all around, it seems to me, to understand that long poems like *Endymion,* *Alastor,* and *The Comedian* can have unrelated themes, and that

---

[18] Outside the poem, Stevens' letter to Hi Simons of 12 January 1940 may also be relevant to the mixing of aesthetic and social themes. Approving Simons' interpretation of *The Comedian* (see n. 1, above) as "correct, not only in the main but in particular, and not only correct but keen," Stevens comments, "I suppose that the way of all mind is from romanticism to realism, to fatalism and then to indifferentism, unless the cycle re-commences and the thing goes from indifferentism back to romanticism all over again." He then goes on, in the next paragraph, to speculate on "a new romanticism"—not the "imaginative realism" that we have come to see as a main theme in Stevens' work generally, but Communism! (*Letters of Wallace Stevens,* pp. 350–351).

[19] *Letters of Wallace Stevens,* p. 294.

we do not, in *reading* them, really object to these unrelatednesses. All three poems were, for their authors, serious efforts, and we read and reread them with a comparable seriousness, responding to their various concerns as they are offered to us. It is only when we write our critical explanations, seeking some neat, unified schematization of the allegory, that such unrelatednesses become a problem. It may be, ultimately, that the reading of long poems and the writing of critical interpretations are totally different classes of activity. If the latter is to be more realistically aligned with the former, we shall have to relax a little in the matter of coherence. I would not go so far as to invoke Keats's description of the long poem (in this instance *Endymion,* when he had just begun writing it) as "a little Region [for readers] to wander in where they may pick and choose" (*Letters,* I, 170). But surely, as a critical value, "unity" is overrated these days.

Keats and Romance:
The "Reality"
of *Isabella*

In "The Fall of Endymion: A Study in Keats's Intellectual Growth,"[1] Glen O. Allen argues on good grounds that a change in Keats's thinking from conviction to doubt concerning the authenticity of the visionary imagination occurred during the winter of 1817–18, when he was completing and revising *Endymion* and copying it out for the printer. Accompanying this change is a growing dissatisfaction with "romance," a tendency that runs through Keats's letters and poems of this winter and in the verse epistle to J. H. Reynolds of 25 March 1818 culminates paradoxically in a tremendous vision of anti-romantic "truth" (he sees "too distinct into the core / Of an eternal fierce destruction") and a closing statement that he will take refuge from such "detested moods in new Romance."[2] I wish to reexamine the "new Romance"—Keats's last large poetic failure, *Isabella*—against the background of this shifting attitude toward romance. *Isabella* is a more complex poem than critics generally allow, and I think it anticipates Keats's major poems of 1819 in ways hitherto not sufficiently remarked.

I

In September 1817 Keats was with Benjamin Bailey at Oxford, reading Wordsworth and composing Book III of *Endymion*. On

[1] *Keats-Shelley Journal*, VI (1957), 37–57.
[2] *The Letters of John Keats*, ed. Hyder E. Rollins (Cambridge, Mass., 1958), I, 262–263.

the 28th, having recently finished Book III, he confided to B. R. Haydon, "My Ideas with respect to it [the poem] . . . are very low—and I would write the subject thoroughly again. but I am tired of it and think the time would be better spent in writing a new Romance which I have in my eye for next summer" (*Letters*, I, 168). His weariness and discontent mounted in the months that followed. Conversation and correspondence with Bailey, serious study of Wordsworth, whom he met in December, and the reading of Fielding and Smollett came together with the ever-present influence of Shakespeare to accelerate his progress toward the "nobler life" that he looked forward to in *Sleep and Poetry*, in which he would treat "the agonies, the strife / Of human hearts" (123-125). The letter to George and Tom of late December 1817, in which he on one day speaks of art's intensity "making all disagreeables evaporate" and on another day writes down the famous definition of Negative Capability, shows a greatly increased awareness of suffering and evil in the world and of the problems of dealing with them in art (*Letters*, I, 192–194). Early in January 1818, in comparing Scott and Smollett, the one endeavoring to throw "so interesting and ramantic a colouring into common and low Characters as to give them a touch of the Sublime," the other pulling down and leveling "what with other Men would continue Romance," Keats expresses a preference for the latter (I, 200). And in a letter to Bailey of the 23rd, he further comments on the inadequacies of romance: "the most skyey Knight errantry" is incompetent to heal human suffering (I, 209).

All this amounts to what Keats refers to when he tells George and Tom, in a later letter of 23 January, "I think a little change has taken place in my intellect lately." As an instance of "a very gradual ripening of the intellectual powers," he copies down the sonnet he wrote on the preceding day, *On Sitting Down to Read King Lear Once Again*:

> O golden tongued Romance with serene Lute!
> Fair plumed syren! [Queen of] far away!

Leave melodizing on this wintry day,
Shut up thine olden volume & be mute.
Adieu! . . .

Romance's serene lute and inappropriate melodizing, as ineffectual and out of date as "skyey Knight errantry," are herewith
banished: "Let me not wander in a barren dream" (*Letters*, I,
214–215). Though he sometimes subsequently calls his poems
"romances" (as in the letter to Haydon quoted above and in the
sonnet *When I have fears*, l. 6), Keats never again wholeheartedly
embraces the *idea* of romance. When he tells his publishers on 21
March that "a ramance is a fine thing notwithstanding the cir-
culating Libraries" (*Letters*, I, 253), he is defending the subtitle of
Endymion; the self-castigation of his Preface, speaking of ferment,
uncertainty, thicksightedness, and mawkishness, shows what he
had come to think of the poem. And like the sonnet on reread-
ing *Lear,* the other short pieces of this period, written at home
and, after the first week of March 1818, at Teignmouth, generally
reflect Keats's intellectual ripening: they stress human mortality
(*In a drear-nighted December* and the *Four Seasons* sonnet), the
contrarieties of life (*Welcome joy, and welcome sorrow*), the
impossibility of escape (*God of the Meridian*), and the differences
between Keats's own situation and that of poets of an earlier,
simpler age (the sonnet to Spenser, *Robin Hood, Lines on the
Mermaid Tavern*).

The verse epistle that he wrote to Reynolds on 25 March 1818,
just before resuming work on *Isabella* (a few stanzas of which
he had composed sometime before leaving town on 4 March), is
a most revealing document concerning Keats's attitude toward
romance (*Letters*, I, 259–263). The first sixty-six lines describe a
series of ridiculous and fantastic dreams that Keats says he had
"as last night I lay in bed"; a middle paragraph (67–85) comments
on the relationship between such dreamings and one's daytime
awareness and concerns; a third section (86–105) tells of a vision

Keats has had of nature's cruelty, "an eternal fierce destruction";
and the concluding lines (105-113) dismiss the whole as "Moods
of one's mind." In the prose following the verses, Keats apologizes
for the "unconnected subject, and careless verse," and Professor
Bate reminds us that we should not approach such impromptu
lines "with formal expectations that are wildly irrelevant" to
Keats's intentions on the occasion.[3] Nevertheless, the paragraph
bridging the fantastic dreams and the account of nature's cruelty
does make sense, and is of considerable interest as representing a
midpoint in Keats's development from the realm of Flora and old
Pan in the poems of 1816-17 to the "nobler life" of the poems of
1819.

> O that our dreamings all of sleep or wake
> Would all their colours from the sunset take:
> From something of material sublime,
> Rather than shadow our own Soul's daytime   70
> In the dark void of Night. For in the world
> We jostle—but my flag is not unfurl'd
> On the Admiral staff—and to philosophize
> I dare not yet!—Oh never will the prize,
> High reason, and the lore of good and ill   75
> Be my award. Things cannot to the will
> Be settled, but they tease us out of thought.
> Or is it that Imagination brought
> Beyond its proper bound, yet still confined,—
> Lost in a sort of Purgatory blind,   80
> Cannot refer to any standard law

[3] Walter Jackson Bate, *John Keats* (Cambridge, Mass., 1963), p. 307. For
recent discussion of the lines, see Albert Gérard, "Romance and Reality:
Continuity and Growth in Keats's View of Art," *Keats-Shelley Journal*, XI
(1962), 19-23 (reprinted in revised form in Gérard's *English Romantic
Poetry*, Berkeley and Los Angeles, 1968, pp. 217-224); and Stuart M.
Sperry, Jr., "Keats's *Epistle to John Hamilton Reynolds*," *ELH*, XXXVI
(1969), 562-574.

Of either earth or heaven?—It is a flaw
In happiness to see beyond our bourn—
It forces us in Summer skies to mourn:
It spoils the singing of the Nightingale.   85

By way of old-fashioned paraphrase, the first five and a half of
these lines may, with a little judicious trimming, be reduced to
the bare statement: "O that our dreamings would all their colours
take from something sublime [= elevated, "uplifted from the
world," ∴ unearthly, like the fantastic dreams of ll. 1–66] rather
than from our own soul's daytime [the mind's or self's everyday
experiences]; for in the world we jostle (and in unearthly dreamings we don't)"—i.e., sublime dreamings are preferable to the
mental repetition of daytime worldly jostling.[4] The reason for
this statement follows in the next five and a half lines (72–77):
Keats has not yet learned to philosophize, to settle problems of
good and evil that arise from our "Soul's daytime" and jostling in
the world; such problems "tease us out of thought," forcing us
back to dreams. But then a new consideration enters with line 78:
sublime dreamings are not satisfactory either; the poet inhabits
the mortal world, and as a consequence his imagination, "still
confined," cannot wholly escape but falls halfway between worlds,
"Lost in a sort of Purgatory blind." Dreaming therefore results
only in unhappiness by creating dissatisfaction (82–85). The upshot is skepticism without any resolution. Mortal men cannot escape to heaven, "Purgatory blind" is not acceptable, and life in
the world is mainly struggle ("jostling" and, in the next verse
paragraph, the "eternal fierce destruction," which may have been
what prompted Keats's ruminations in the first place). The lines
expound the insufficiencies of dreaming and Keats's inability to
find any suitable alternative way of confronting problems in the
world. They do not seem a very auspicious preliminary to *Isabella*,

[4] Cf. the 1807 text of Wordsworth's *To H. C.*, ll. 28–29, "Not doom'd
to jostle with unkindly shocks; / Or to be trail'd along the soiling earth."

the "new Romance" that Keats says he will "Take refuge" in
(111–112), which he completed a month later.[5]

II

Although it has received both very high praise (by Richard
Woodhouse, Reynolds, Lamb, Arnold, and the Pre-Raphaelites)
and blame (by Keats and practically everyone else), there is less
variety in the criticism of *Isabella* than in that of any other long
poem by Keats.[6] Standard procedure is first to condemn the sentimentality, mawkishness, and vulgarity—all the qualities we
call Huntian—then to admire Keats's idealization of the lovers
in the first half of the poem and some of the stronger stanzas of

---

[5] Keats began *Isabella* sometime after 3 February, if the project of mod-
ernizing Boccaccio was in fact suggested by Hazlitt's lecture of that evening (see Hazlitt's *Complete Works*, ed. P. P. Howe, London, 1930–34, V,
82; Rollins' chronology in *Letters*, I, 39, has Keats attending on the 3rd,
but the sole evidence is Keats's statement of eighteen days—and two lectures—later: "I hear Hazlitt's Lectures regularly," I, 237). He wrote "the
first few stanzas" before departing for Teignmouth on 4 March, and had
"the rest here finish'd" on 27 April (*Letters*, I, 274). From the reference
to a "new Romance" at the end of the epistle to Reynolds, Bate, p. 310,
infers that most of the poem was written between 25 March and 27 April.
Aileen Ward, *John Keats: The Making of a Poet* (New York, 1963), p.
428, has an informative note on the possibility of revisions and additions
to the poem later in the year.

[6] Among older critics, M. R. Ridley, *Keats' Craftsmanship* (Oxford,
1933), pp. 18–56, provides the most thoroughgoing enumeration of the
poem's lapses in taste, grammar, and meaning; Sidney Colvin, *John Keats:
His Life and Poetry . . .* (New York, 1925), pp. 389–396, is the poem's
most eloquent defender; Claude Lee Finney, *The Evolution of Keats's Poetry* (Cambridge, Mass., 1936), I, 371–379, offers substantial background
information; and Herbert G. Wright, *Boccaccio in England from Chaucer
to Tennyson* (London, 1957), pp. 397–407, considers in detail the relationship of the poem to Keats's principal source, the fifth edition (1684) of a
1620 English translation perhaps by John Florio (see n. 11, below). Among
recent work, Bate's discussion of the poem's "continued defiance of general
criticism," pp. 310–315, is valuable. The critical comments most directly
relevant to my own view of the poem are those by Priestley and Ward
quoted in the next paragraph.

description in the latter half (e.g., XXVII, XXXVI–XXXVII, XLV, LIII), and finally to call the poem "transitional" and rush on to *Hyperion* and *The Eve of St. Agnes*. The main attitude is puzzlement: why this retrogression to stylistic habits that Keats should by now have outgrown (and in a letter of 3 February declared he had outgrown—*Letters,* I, 223–225), and why this reversion to romance just when his mind was filled with the idea of the uselessness of romance for any other purpose than escape? As Douglas Bush puts it, "It seems strange that the author of the sonnet on *King Lear* and the *Epistle to Reynolds* could, in the same few months, produce *Isabella*." [7]

This strangeness can be modified somewhat by a reassessment of Keats's intentions. Critics do notice realistic details among the sentimental. F. E. L. Priestley, for instance, studying the influence of Chaucer, sees in the poem "an attempt to present the psychology of a character, and . . . an effort, not always successful, but in the digging scene decidedly so, to create a strong impression of pathos by realistic simplicity." [8] Aileen Ward comments that a "string of images of medicine and disease runs through the poem like a dark vein through marble—a description of Isabella as thin and pale as a young mother with a sick child; accounts of stifling and pulsing and hallucinations and fever; pharmaceutical lore of distilling and compounding, of poisonous flowers and strong potions; observations of haemorrhage, psychological shock, and consumption; a metaphor of amputation; and, finally, a detailed picture of a freshly exhumed corpse. . . . This imagery implies a more direct confrontation of reality than Keats had yet made in his poetry." [9] I would inquire further into the purpose of these realistic details. There are many of them, and taken together I think they allow a new view of *Isabella* as *anti*-romance—in the

[7] Douglas Bush, ed., *John Keats: Selected Poems and Letters* (Boston, 1959), p. 329.
[8] "Keats and Chaucer," *Modern Language Quarterly,* V (1944), 443.
[9] Ward, p. 174.

second half, at least, a tough-minded "modern" recasting of what Keats came to realize was a kind of naïve romance more appropriate to an age gone by, "The simple plaining of a minstrel's song."

There are many evidences of the practical side of Keats's mind at work—in stanzas XII and XIII, for example, where (in images later reversed in *Ode on Melancholy*) we are reminded that the famous lovers of "doleful stories" did, after all, enjoy happiness, and that we waste too much pity on them in thinking only of their subsequent misfortunes; in the canceled stanza following XVII, where Keats attempts to explain the brothers' avariciousness as the result of mathematical dreams that their mother had "In the longing time"; [10] in stanzas XXX and XXXI, linking love and selfishness; in stanza XXXIX, describing Lorenzo's loneliness in death, the final separation from humanity; in stanza XLV, in which Keats imagines "scull, coffin'd bones, and funeral stole" of each rotting corpse buried in the churchyard. The early frequency of the images of disease that Professor Ward has noticed—"malady" (4), "sick longing" (23), "cheeks paler" (26), "Fell sick" (34), "Fell thin" (35), "ill" (37), "Fever'd" (46), "very pale and dead" (53)—suggests that Keats may have been setting up a contrast between the innocent courtly lovesickness of the first part of the tale and the genuine sickness and death that follow. But to get immediately to the point of my interpretation I shall concentrate on some of the grisly details toward the end of the poem that Keats describes as "wormy circumstance" (385).

In apologizing to Boccaccio "For venturing syllables that ill beseem / The quiet glooms of such a piteous theme" (151–152)— i.e., for portraying the brothers' commercial character at too great length in the anti-capitalist stanzas XIV–XVIII—Keats insists that he is not attempting "To make old prose in modern rhyme more sweet" (156). Once Lorenzo is slain, however, this straightforward

[10] *The Poetical Works of John Keats,* ed. H. W. Garrod, 2nd ed. (Oxford, 1958), p. 221.

disclaimer becomes understatement, as may be seen by comparing the "old prose" with Keats's increasingly *less* "sweet" modernization. The earlier account of Isabella's vision begins as follows: "she fell into a Trance or Sleep, and dreamed that the Ghost of *Lorenzo* appeared unto her, in torn and unbefitting Garments, his looks pale, meager, and starving."[11] Keats enlarges on the physical details, adding among other things an impairment of voice and dirt in the ears:

> the forest tomb
> Had marr'd his glossy hair which once could shoot
> Lustre into the sun, and put cold doom
> Upon his lips, and taken the soft lute
> From his lorn voice, and past his loamed ears
> Had made a miry channel for his tears.   (275–280)

He repeats the idea of physical marring ten stanzas later: "Who hath not loiter'd in a green church-yard, / And let his spirit . . . Work through the clayey soil . . . Pitying each form that hungry Death hath marr'd . . . ?" (353–357). And near the end of the story, where in his source the brothers had uncovered the head and found it "not so much consumed, but by the Locks of Hair, they knew it to be *Lorenzo*'s," Keats chooses to emphasize corruption: Lorenzo's face has become a "thing . . . vile with green and livid spot" (475).

Keats makes several interesting changes in the digging scene. The old prose translation has Isabella and her nurse riding "directly to the designed place, which being covered with some store of dryed leaves, and more deeply sunk than any other part of the Ground thereabout, they digged not far, but they found the body of the murthered *Lorenzo*, as yet very little corrupted or impaired." Keats's heroine is made to work a good deal harder: "with her knife . . . she began / To dig more fervently than

---

[11] Here and below I quote from the translation that Keats used, *The Novels and Tales of the Renowned John Boccacio*, 5th ed. (London, 1684), pp. 182–185.

misers can" (367–368); then the old nurse "put her lean hands to the horrid thing," and for "Three hours"—the one digging with the knife, the other clawing with bare hands—"they labour'd at this travail sore" (381–382). In the old prose, after Isabella comes upon the body,

Gladly would she have carried the whole body with her, secretly to bestow honourable Enterment on it, but yet exceeded the compass of her Ability. Wherefore, in regard she could not have all, yet she would be possessed of a part, and having brought a keen Razor with her, by help of the Nurse, she divided the Head from the Body, wrapped it up in a Napkin, which the Nurse conveyed into her Lap, and then laid the Body in the Ground again. This being undiscovered by any, they departed thence, and arrived at home in convenient time. . . .

"Divided the Head from the Body," especially in conjunction with "keen Razor," connotes a surgical tidiness that Keats the surgeon chose to forgo. Without repeating any of the source's quite reasonable explanation for their action, he proceeds directly to the action itself: "With duller steel than the Perséan sword / They cut away" Lorenzo's head (393–394). Presumably *all* "steel" is duller than the sword with which Perseus in one blow severed the Medusa's head. Why, then, this special emphasis on dullness, with its suggestion of prolonged sawing or perhaps clumsy hacking at the neck? Like the lengthening of time ("Three hours") and the addition of the nurse's barehanded digging, this "duller steel" makes more realistic and, owing to the nature of the business, more gruesome the unemotional bare bones of the story Keats was recasting.

In the midst of the exhumation, between the three hours' digging and the severing of the head, Keats asks a question that may already have occurred to some readers:

> Ah! wherefore all this wormy circumstance?
> Why linger at the yawning tomb so long?

> O for the gentleness of old Romance,
>   The simple plaining of a minstrel's song!
> Fair reader, at the old tale take a glance,
>   For here, in truth, it doth not well belong
> To speak:—O turn thee to the very tale,
> And taste the music of that vision pale.   (385–392)

The lines again stress the general difference between "old prose" and "modern rhyme" mentioned earlier in the apostrophe to Boccaccio (156). But the reader who now glances at the old tale can see a specific difference that may well be a main point of Keats's modernization. To Boccaccio's original heading, which includes a brief summary of the story, the English translation adds the following explanation: "Wherein is plainly proved, That Love cannot be rooted up, by any Humane Power or Providence; especially in such a Soul, where it hath been really apprehended." Keats refers to this statement of theme or "moral" in his next stanza:

>   The ancient harps have said,
> Love never dies, but lives, immortal Lord:
>   If Love impersonate was ever dead,
> Pale Isabella kiss'd it, and low moan'd.
> 'Twas love; cold,—dead indeed, but not dethroned.
>   (396–400)

He has already told us, at the point at which the brothers murdered Lorenzo, "There in that forest did his great love cease" (218). The issue is clouded a little later when Isabella, in her vision of Lorenzo, connects his paleness with a spiritualization of love and imagines him saying that he feels "A greater love through all my essence steal" (320). But here the emphasis is again on deadness. "Love impersonate" is Lorenzo's severed head, and the final lines of the stanza say, in effect, that no love was ever more dead than the love Isabella kissed.[12]

---

[12] Keats's wording and syntax in ll. 398–399 are perhaps a little confusing, but a holograph version of l. 398—"If ever any piece of love was dead"

If "love; cold,—dead indeed, but not dethroned" (400) seems
at odds with the ancient harps' maxim that "Love never dies, but
lives, immortal Lord" (397), there is good reason; for in Keats's
poem love is "not dethroned" only in what is by now a very sick
mind. Still another difference between Keats's source and his
poem has to do with the point at which the heroine goes mad. In
the old prose it is almost at the end of the story that Isabella's
neighbors notice "incessant weeping" and "violent oppressions" as
she carries the pot of basil around with her. In the poem we see
symptoms much earlier—for example, in Isabella's Hamlet-like
reaction after the vision of Lorenzo, "Ha! ha!" (329), and in the
"feverous hectic flame" and burning smile that the nurse observes
when Isabella, "after looking round the champaign wide, / Shows
her a knife" (347–350). And now, in the stanzas following the
statement that love was "dead indeed, but not dethroned," Isabella
is depicted as fully deranged. She combs the hair of the severed
head, points the eyelashes, washes away dirt with her tears, continues kissing—"and still she comb'd, and kept / Sighing all day—
and still she kiss'd, and wept" (403–408). Wrapping the head in a
scarf, she puts it in a garden pot and sets a basil plant over it.
And from this point on, she entirely shuts out the objective world
around her, ignoring some of the "Things real—such as existences
of Sun Moon & Stars" that Keats had recently discussed in a letter
to Bailey, 13 March 1818 (*Letters*, I, 242–243):

> And she forgot the stars, the moon, and sun,
>   And she forgot the blue above the trees,
> And she forgot the dells where waters run,
>   And she forgot the chilly autumn breeze;
> She had no knowledge when the day was done,
>   And the new morn she saw not: but in peace
> Hung over her sweet basil evermore,
> And moisten'd it with tears unto the core.   (417–424)

(*The Poetical Works of John Keats,* p. 231)—makes the intention clear
enough.

Herbert G. Wright, whose investigation of Keats's use of his source results in a somewhat different view of the poem from the one offered here, compares Isabella, in these lines "lamenting her loss in a bleak setting that harmonises with her grief," with Wordsworth's heroine in *The Thorn*.[13] One could follow this up, noting the occurrence of "O misery!" early in Keats's poem (235) and the vague resemblance of Isabella's "burthen"—"O cruelty, / To steal my basil-pot away from me!" (503–504)—to the refrain in Wordsworth's poem, "Oh misery! oh misery! / Oh woe is me! oh misery!" Other Wordsworthian elements include the wild eyes of Lorenzo's ghost (289), the direct address to "Fair reader" (389 ff.), and of course the general emphasis on simplicity and the grim matter-of-factness of all the "wormy circumstance." What is most Wordsworthian of all is the interest in psychology that dominates the latter half of the poem. In focusing on Isabella's progressive derangement, Keats was, whether he knew it or not, tracing "the primary laws of our nature: chiefly, as far as regards the manner in which we associate ideas in a state of excitement." [14] And it was in *Isabella,* for all its floweriness of language, that he came closest to writing a lyrical ballad.

With Isabella's complete separation from the physical world, Keats has come a considerable distance from the beginning of his poem, where fair Isabella and the worshipful young Lorenzo were suffering all the agonies of high romantic love—"some stir of heart, some malady," with dreams and nightly weeping (1–8). Courtly love has given place to psychology, lovesickness has become real sickness, and romance has been put down by the realism of "wormy circumstance." "The simple plaining of a minstrel's song," Keats is saying, is no longer appropriate to the wintry-day "modernity" of 1818: "For here, in truth, it doth not well belong / To speak" (388–391).

[13] Wright, p. 407.
[14] Preface to the second edition of *Lyrical Ballads*.

III

Speculating on the origins of the poem, I would suggest that *Isabella* really begins with a letter of 3 February 1818 in which Keats thanks Reynolds for two sonnets and comments on their style. "All I can say is that where there are a throng of delightful Images ready drawn simplicity is the only thing." Sentimentality and obtrusiveness, poetic brooding and peacocking of moderns like Hunt and Wordsworth, are to be avoided: "We must cut this, and not be rattlesnaked into any more of the like. . . . Let us have the old Poets, & robin Hood" (*Letters,* I, 223–225). On the evening of this same day, 3 February, Hazlitt in a lecture suggested the translating of the story of Isabella and some others, and Keats certainly heard about the lecture if he did not actually attend. I think it was in the mood of the letter to Reynolds that he began writing the poem. "Simplicity," his term for the plainness and artlessness of earlier life and literature,[15] "is the only thing." Whether or not he was consciously imitating the "old Poets," his heroine in the opening line is "poor simple Isabel," and the first half of the poem, describing the lovers' passions and miseries, has a simplicity that is at bottom the cause of many of our objections concerning the style. In the course of composing, however, he must have become aware, just as in the verse epistle to Reynolds, that where human suffering and "the lore of good and ill" are concerned, the simplicity of old leaves too many things out of the picture. Wordsworth, with or without the brooding and peacocking, was the better guide after all. The result of this turn of thinking is the cool look at the realities of romance that we get in the second half of the poem. "Simple Isabel" near the end (446) has gone mad, and her simplicity now

---

[15] E.g., in "Oh! what a power hath white simplicity" (*This pleasant tale is like a little copse,* l. 9) and "O, give me their old vigour, and . . . my song should die away / Content as theirs, / Rich in the simple worship of a day" (*Ode to May,* ll. 9–14).

manifests itself in forgetting "the stars, the moon, and sun," a separation soon to be made permanent by death. Keats is no longer stammering where old Boccaccio used to sing.

Obviously the poem looks forward to subsequent developments in Keats's brief career. Less than a year later, in the fifth stanza of *The Eve of St. Agnes* he describes "the argent revelry, / With plume, tiara, and all rich array, / Numerous as shadows haunting fairily / The brain, new stuff'd, in youth, with triumphs gay / Of old romance" (37-41). When he then says "These let us wish away," he is of course turning from the revelers to focus on Madeline and get his story under way; but he is also wishing away the "triumphs gay / Of old romance." Porphyro's conquest of Madeline is, at a glance at least, one of those romantic triumphs, but it is not very gay, and Keats introduced realistic details into the narrative that cast doubt on the morality of Porphyro's "stratagem" and condemn Madeline's pursuit of a ritual so far that she loses touch with reality. "Old romance" does not dominate any of the subsequent completed poems. The fact is that, from about the middle of *Isabella* on, Keats's constant sense of the insufficiencies of romance is—I hope no longer paradoxically—one of his chief qualities as a major English Romantic poet. A look at what Keats called "the reality" of *Isabella* (*Letters,* II, 174) not only makes that poem more interesting but opens the way for a better understanding of the poems toward which it points, the anti-romances and ultimately skeptical lyrics of 1819 that put Keats "among the English Poets."

"The Heart and Nature of Man" in *Hyperion, Lamia,* and *The Fall of Hyperion*

> The aim of the dreamer, after all, is merely to go on dreaming and not to be molested by the world. His dreams are his protection against the world. But the aims of life are antithetical to those of the dreamer, and the teeth of the world are sharp.
>
> * * *
>
> "What," asked Cass, unexpectedly, *"does* one replace a dream with? I wish I knew." . . .
>
> "I suppose," said Ida, in an extraordinary voice, "that one replaces a dream with reality."
>
> Everybody laughed, nervously. . . .
>
> "Only," said Ida, "that's not so easy to do." [1]

Hyperion, Lamia, and *The Fall of Hyperion*—among Keats's major achievements the three longest pieces after *Endymion*—have been so thoroughly discussed by critics in recent years that there would seem to be nothing new to offer in aid of explication. I wish, however, to consider the relationship of these works to the rest of Keats's poems, and very briefly to point out the difference between Keats's having and not having something important to say concerning "the agonies, the strife / Of human hearts," the large subject that he was working his way toward ever since he announced his plan in *Sleep and Poetry*. My epigraph from Baldwin's novel will serve as well as any other to suggest what elsewhere in this volume I have taken to be Keats's

[1] James Baldwin, *Another Country* (New York, 1962), pp. 199, 357-358.

46

central preoccupation in his writings from *Endymion* on through 1819, his peculiar focus on the human heart's capacity to invest in a "dream" (or dream-like illusion of some sort) and then, not invariably to replace it with a reality, but to experience the inevitable necessity of such a replacement. This preoccupation is the main business of *Lamia,* but is totally absent from what we have of *Hyperion* and presumably also from what was, after the introduction, to be the substance of *The Fall of Hyperion.* I do not judge the Hyperion fragments to be inferior because they fail to incorporate Keats's principal theme. But *Lamia* is a finished work and the fragments are fragments, and I should like to speculate on the possible connection of these facts with the presence and absence, respectively, of the theme in the three works.

I

It is notable that while *Hyperion* has deservedly been acclaimed for its stylistic achievement and for its impressive statement of what look like some very significant ideas—especially the doctrine of historical progress in Oceanus' eloquent speech in Book II and the account of the deification of Apollo at the end of the fragment—it is seldom successfully integrated with the rest of Keats's writings in a view of what the major poems, taken as a whole, are all about. In the works of a different sort of poet (Byron, for example) this would not be much of a problem, and I do not urge that thematic relatedness of poems is axiomatically desirable or that it should be a criterion for evaluation. But it is a demonstrable fact that Keats's best writings, like Wordsworth's, constitute a unified and coherent body of work; one can pick poems at random (e.g., *I wandered lonely as a cloud* and *The Solitary Reaper,* or *The Eve of Saint Mark* and *Ode on Melancholy*), and nearly always relate one to the other, showing how they essentially deal with the same thing. This is not true of *Hyperion,* which, for all its astonishing epic resplendence, just sits there apart from the rest, like Saturn himself, "quiet as a

stone" (I.4), almost as if it had been written by someone other
than Keats (the Shelley of *Prometheus Unbound,* for example,
except of course for the quite *un*Shelleyan concreteness observable
in much of Keats's fragment). I would suggest that this lack of
relatedness has a bearing both on Keats's abandonment of the
fragment and on the lack of critical agreement about what he
was trying to do in the work.

The specific interpretive problems in the poem have to do
chiefly with the question of where Keats's sympathy lies in the
contest between the Titans and the Olympian gods; with the
apparent confusion (just as in *Prometheus Unbound* and Byron's
Manfred, to cite parallel cases) concerning who has power over
whom, and why; with the significance of the various comparisons made between the gods' and human affairs; [2] and especially
with the relationship of the deification of Apollo in Book III to
the war between the gods that is the subject of Books I and II.
The critics have, of course, attempted to explain and reconcile
these things, but even at their best they frequently seem unwilling or unable to take into consideration all of the principal elements in the fragment, concentrating on, say, Saturn's loss of
identity or Oceanus' speech or the exchange between Mnemosyne
and Apollo, and sometimes coming up with rather unKeatsian
concerns like social theory or some opposition of abstractions as
a key to the whole.[3] Relatively few critics will allow that Keats

[2] See I.42–44, 49–51, 159–160, 169–175, 183, 185, 198–200, 253–254, 333–
335; II.96–97, 101–104.

[3] Virtually every major Keats critic has written on the work. Among recent writers I would single out Walter Jackson Bate, *John Keats* (Cambridge, Mass., 1963), pp. 388–417 (for valuable general discussion); Walter
H. Evert, *Aesthetic and Myth in the Poetry of Keats* (Princeton, 1965), pp.
225–243 (for a convincing explanation—to an extent followed in the present
essay—of why Keats abandoned the fragment); and Brian Wilkie, *Romantic Poets and Epic Tradition* (Madison and Milwaukee, 1965), pp. 145–187
(for the most comprehensive discussion in print taking the fragment as a
unified whole).

left off the poem because (like Coleridge in *Christabel*) he had no clear thematic purpose in mind.

Keats first conceived of his earlier long mythological poem, *Endymion,* while writing the latest of the pieces published in *Poems* of 1817. The main themes of *Endymion*—sympathetic identification, self and solitude versus humanitarian activities, the opposition between mundane reality and some ideal or immortal existence, the question of the "truth" of imagination—are all topics that he was pondering and writing about in letters and shorter poems at the time and earlier; and for each of these themes, Keats's treatment was as full and definitive as he could make it when he wrote the poem. *Hyperion,* though drafted a year or more after the completion of *Endymion,* in the closing months of 1818 and the spring of 1819, was initially thought of while Keats was working on *Endymion.* In his letters he first refers to the Hyperion project by name on 23 January 1818, when he tells B. R. Haydon that "the nature of *Hyperion* will lead me to treat it in a more naked and grecian Manner—and the march of passion and endeavour will be undeviating—and one great contrast between them will be—that the Hero of the written tale [Endymion] being mortal is led on, like Buonaparte, by circumstance; whereas the Apollo in Hyperion being a fore-seeing God will shape his actions like one." [4] Keats does not write as if the project were just then a new one, and Walter Evert, adding his own observations to some of Ernest de Selincourt and finding allusions to *Hyperion* in all four books of *Endymion,* suggests that "the idea of *Hyperion* was at least latent as far back as late August 1817" and possibly some months earlier: "references to [*Hyperion*] . . . appear in *Endymion* at every stage of its devel-

[4] *The Letters of John Keats,* ed. Hyder E. Rollins (Cambridge, Mass., 1958), I, 207. The mention on 28 September 1817 of "a new Romance which I have in my eye for next summer" (I, 168) probably also refers to *Hyperion.*

opment."[5] On the evidence at hand, it is clear that Keats planned *Hyperion* more than a year before he actually began writing it, and at the very time he was engrossed in *Endymion*. It is also clear that he originally conceived of *Hyperion* in terms of the same elements he was working with in *Endymion*—the style would be different, as he told Haydon ("a more naked and grecian Manner"), as well as the chief characters' motivation ("circumstance" vs. self-shaping), but his starting intention, in a long narrative poem "to try once more" to re-create "the beautiful mythology of Greece" (as he wrote in the Preface to *Endymion*), was basically the same in both poems. *Endymion,* however, in embodying definitively (for the time) all the things that he cared most about when he wrote the poem, represented both a culmination and an emptying-out. What was there left to do in *Hyperion?*

As everyone recognizes by now, the period between the completion of the first draft of *Endymion* in November 1817 and the beginning of the actual writing of *Hyperion* in September 1818 was crucial in Keats's mental development. Practically all the recoverable activities and experiences—his reading in Shakespeare, Wordsworth, and the eighteenth-century novel; the realistic tendencies of his verse epistle to J. H. Reynolds, *Isabella,* and a number of shorter poems; his speculations on poetry and life in the letters (especially the idea of "sharpening one's vision into the heart and nature of Man—of convincing ones nerves that the World is full of Misery and Heartbreak, Pain, Sickness and oppression" in the letter to Reynolds of 3 May 1818, *Letters,* I, 281); his impressions during the walking tour with Charles Brown in the summer; the mortal illness of his brother Tom (who died on 1 December)—point to a rapidly growing knowledge of human suffering and the need to get on with his progress toward writing about "the agonies, the strife / Of human hearts." By the time he began *Hyperion* he was ready to deal with *human* char-

[5] Evert, pp. 227–229.

acters, as he had in *Isabella* and shortly would do in *The Eve of St. Agnes, The Eve of Saint Mark,* and the odes.

But Keats, though he has been described as "a man of fits and starts," [6] was characteristically unwilling to give up a project once it was under way: he completed his course in medical school, even though he knew he did not want to practice as an apothecary or surgeon; he completed *Endymion,* even though he became weary of it long before he finished; and up to a point he went on with *Hyperion.* According to the scheme of 1817–18, *Hyperion* was to be about the gods—and so it is, the only major poem of Keats that has no mortal characters (Apollo is of course supposed to be something other than a god before he is deified, but we do not identify him as a mortal). The many comparisons with mundane affairs in the poem, and the deification of Apollo through the envisioning of "Knowledge enormous" of what we take (seemingly for good reason in view of the parallel experience of the poet-dreamer in *The Fall of Hyperion*) to be human misery, represent elements that, although present, were not prominent in *Endymion* and, I should guess, were not included in the original plan for the epic. But these elements are not successfully merged with the more obvious mythological and historical concerns of the fragment. It is true that Books I and II deal with inevitable change and the characters' reactions to it [7]— shock, disbelief, acquiescence, rationalizing, rage—and Book III may have been intended to portray Apollo (and by easy interpretation the mature poet) as witness to this inevitable change. It is also true that change is a central fact of human life. But Keats depicts change at such a lofty and abstract level that, just

[6] By the publisher J. A. Hessey (Edmund Blunden, *Keats's Publisher,* London, 1936, p. 56).

[7] "The overwhelming knowledge—the joy and tragic loss—of inevitable change" (Bate, p. 391, who in several other places, thinking of Apollo in Book III, says that *Hyperion* is primarily about the growth of human consciousness).

as in *Prometheus Unbound,* which is also ostensibly about human affairs, men and their problems seem relegated to a very minor place, almost as if they were incidental interests. The upshot is that, while some of the lines of *Hyperion* do touch on the agonies and strife of human hearts, the bulk of the fragment fundamentally does not. Keats was embarked on a long epic poem whose principal subject was not miles but literally a whole realm apart from what he had most on his mind at the time. It is not difficult to see this conflict of concerns—the commitment to the original plan of writing about gods when he really wanted to write about men and women—as a main fact behind his abandonment of the work in the spring of 1819. The "Knowledge enormous" that Apollo arrives at in Book III should have made Keats set aside the fragment. And so he did.

II

Lamia, which Keats wrote in July–September 1819, close to a year after beginning the composition of *Hyperion,* is an entirely different sort of poem, quite aside from the fact that it is complete. While there are gods and other non-human creatures in it (Hermes, the nymph, Lamia), there are also human characters (Lycius, Apollonius, the people of Corinth), and Keats very definitely has a purpose and a theme in this poem in a way that he did not in *Hyperion.*

Lamia is one of the results of a several-months-long burst of creativity that had begun with *The Eve of St. Agnes* and had also produced (to name only the best-known poems) *La Belle Dame sans Merci* and at least three of the great odes, *To Psyche, To a Nightingale,* and *On a Grecian Urn,* and probably also a fourth, *On Melancholy.* It does not take much, but nevertheless takes a little, critical help to see these works as centering on the dream-reality opposition suggested in my epigraph from Baldwin, with dreaming as a metaphor for investment in a visionary ideal. In these works of the first half of 1819 Keats had gone back to a main theme of *Endymion,* but with a significant change of attitude and a much enlarged recognition of the complexities of the theme. This time, however, he had not exhausted the theme (as in 1818 he had seemingly used up all his ideas in *Endymion,* leaving him nothing new to say when he attempted to write another long poem, *Hyperion,* on the same mythological scheme). There was still room to treat head-on what he had been touching and dealing less directly with in the poems of the preceding six months, and the brief story of Lycius and Lamia in Burton's *Anatomy,* which calls Lamia a "phantasm" and their palace furnishings "no substance but mere illusions," provided an excellent starting point for his fullest and most pessimistic exposition of the dangers of dreaming, of overinvestment in illusion, and the impossibility of escape from the realities of the human condition. In spite of the considerable critical disagreement over Keats's purpose in the poem,[8] *Lamia* is quite explicit in saying what it is about.

The first 145 lines of Part I (which sometimes in the past have been thought extraneous to the narrative, on the grounds that, since Keats merely wanted to transform Lamia from serpent to womanly form, he should have done it in less space) establish the poem's concern with the nature and reality of dreams.[9] When Lamia renders the nymph visible to Hermes, the narrator remarks:

> It was no dream; or say a dream it was,
> Real are the dreams of Gods, and smoothly pass
> Their pleasures in a long immortal dream.   (I.126–128)

[8] See Charles I. Patterson, Jr., *The Dæmonic in the Poetry of John Keats* (Urbana, 1970), pp. 185–188, for a convenient summary of critical interpretations. In general, I follow David Perkins, *The Quest for Permanence* (Cambridge, Mass., 1959), p. 273: "the poem is largely about the consequences of being a dreamer."

[9] Forms of "dream" as noun and verb occur twelve times in the poem, eleven times in Part I, and just once—but very significantly (Lycius' "Begone, foul dream!")—in Part II.

These lines, plus the final comment on Hermes and the nymph as they go into the forest and out of the poem—"Into the green-recessed woods they flew; / Nor grew they pale, as mortal lovers do" (I.144–145)—make plain (certainly they do in retrospect) what the poem is going to be about, and set up a crucial difference between gods and men. For gods dreams are a reality, and by implication for men dreams are not; gods "pass / Their pleasures in a long immortal dream," but mortals merely grow pale instead (or worse, they "waste . . . to a shade," I.270)—and the hero of this poem, like Madeline in *The Eve of St. Agnes*, the knight in *La Belle Dame*, and the speakers in the odes, is unluckily a mortal. Keats had been writing about attempted unions of human and non-human beings at least since the sonnet *Had I a man's fair form*,[10] and had made them the central quests in *Endymion*, *La Belle Dame*, and *Ode to a Nightingale*; even in *The Eve of St. Agnes*, which has only human characters, he invests his hero, Porphyro, with both godly and fairy attributes, so as to set up, for a part of the poem at least, the same kind of mixed pairing. The mortal-nonmortal union is a perfect vehicle for the dreamer's attempt to escape his mortal condition, and the realistic impossibility of such a union guarantees the exposure of the illusion he pursues. Where Keats is considering only immortals—Hermes and the nymph, or the gods in *Hyperion*—there are no strict rules, and dreams can be called "reality"; but in the poem at hand he drops Hermes and the nymph, and focuses on Lycius and Lamia.

The early description of Lamia, in terms progressively more evil, as seeming "at once, some penanced lady elf, / Some demon's mistress, or the demon's self" (I.55–56), and the account of her transformation, which involves convulsions, foaming at the mouth, and a reduction of qualities until "Nothing but pain and ugliness were left" (I.164), do not augur well for the union

[10] See J. Burke Severs, "Keats's Fairy Sonnet," *Keats-Shelley Journal,* VI (1957), 109–113.

about to take place. Nor do the ironic lines early addressed by the narrator to "happy" Lycius:

> Ah, happy Lycius!—for she was a maid
> More beautiful than ever twisted braid,
> Or sigh'd, or blush'd, or on spring-flowered lea
> Spread a green kirtle to the minstrelsy:
> A virgin purest lipp'd, yet in the lore
> Of love deep learned to the red heart's core:
> Not one hour old, yet of sciential brain
> To unperplex bliss from its neighbour pain;
> Define their pettish limits, and estrange
> Their points of contact, and swift counterchange;
> Intrigue with the specious chaos, and dispart
> Its most ambiguous atoms with sure art. . . .
>
> (I.185–196)

Keats criticism has come a long way since M. R. Ridley dismissed the last six lines of this quotation as having "a specious appearance of reflective profundity, and in fact mean[ing] as nearly as may be exactly nothing." [11] Nowadays anyone even half aware of Keats's various statements on the inseparability of pleasure and pain [12] will recognize that something is wrong in these lines. It is a nice trick to be both "A virgin purest lipp'd" and one "in the lore / Of love deep learned to the red heart's core," or to be less than an hour old and "yet of sciential brain"; it is equally nice, and equally impossible for mortals, to separate "bliss from its neighbour pain" and, even while admitting their

[11] *Keats' Craftsmanship* (Oxford, 1933), p. 255. See John Middleton Murry, *Keats* (London, 1955), p. 246.

[12] The most famous is in *Ode on Melancholy,* ll. 21–26. See also, e.g., *Endymion,* II.366 ("fairest joys give most unrest"); *Welcome joy, and welcome sorrow* (the whole poem); *Isabella,* l. 104 ("there is richest juice in poison-flowers"); *The Eve of St. Agnes,* ll. 240, 242 (the *un*natural implications of "Blissfully haven'd both from joy and pain . . . Blinded alike from sunshine and from rain"). The idea is implied in a number of oxymorons in the poems—e.g., "pleasant pain" (*Ode to Psyche,* l. 52) and "sweet unrest" (*Bright star,* l. 12).

"contact, and swift counterchange," to hope to set limits between them. The mortal Lycius' doom is already fixed in the first two hundred lines of the poem.

Perhaps Lycius deserves his fate (certainly in Part II the narrator thinks he does), for the first description characterizes him as a person already highly susceptible to illusion. He is just returning from a religious sacrifice, and now walks along "Thoughtless," until "His phantasy was lost, where reason fades, / In the calm'd twilight of Platonic shades" (I.234-236); like the hoodwinked Madeline as we first see her in *The Eve of St. Agnes,* oblivious of her actual surroundings, he is "shut up in mysteries, / His mind wrapp'd like his mantle" (I.241-242). Ready to fall in love with an illusion, he is immediately smitten when Lamia speaks to him. After he faints upon being told that she is an immortal, and therefore cannot live in his world, Lamia "Put her new lips to his, and gave afresh / The life she had so tangled in her mesh"; his reviving is described as an awakening "from one trance . . . Into another" (I.294-297). From this point on, Lycius is under a magical spell until he is made to see the reality at the end. But, though "blinded" (I.347), he is also partly aware of the illusion he is involved in. When he meets the agent of reality in the poem, Apollonius, who is a harmless enough character when first introduced—in Lycius' own words "sage," a "trusty guide," a "good instructor"—Lycius thinks of him as "The ghost of folly haunting my sweet dreams" (I.375-377), and he shrinks and tries to hide from him. And early in Part II he confesses that he has all along considered Lamia "Not mortal, but of heavenly progeny" (II.87). It is not just the illusion but the mortal elements of vanity and perversity in Lycius that bring about his death.

The sad conclusion of the story is foretold as early as I.260— "Even as thou vanishest so I shall die"—and affirmed again at the end of Part I ("what woe afterwards befel," I.395) and the beginning of Part II ("Had Lycius liv'd . . . ," II.7). Having

committed himself to the inevitability of the outcome, the narrator now begins to feel sorry for his characters and to participate
sympathetically in the goings-on.[13] The result, as many critics
have noted, is a further humanizing of both Lycius and Lamia.
When a "thrill / Of trumpets" reminds him of "the noisy world
almost forsworn" (II.27-33), Lycius *thinks,*[14] and his thought
leads to a reassertion of his human nature: "What mortal hath
a prize, that other men / May be confounded and abash'd
withal, / But lets it sometimes pace abroad majestical, / And tri-
umph . . ." (II.57-60). He insists on holding a wedding feast
to show off his bride before the people of Corinth, and, in the
little domestic conflict of wills that follows between them, Lamia
takes on increasingly the characteristics of a mortal woman—"She
burnt, she lov'd the tyranny, / And, all subdued, consented . . ."
(II.81-82)—with such effect that by the end of the poem trusty
Apollonius has become a villain, and the "tender-person'd Lamia"
a genuine loss when he causes her to "melt into a shade" (II.238).
But however much the narrator enters into the action, we must,
as Walter Evert reminds us,[15] keep in mind that Lamia is still
basically an evil character, a snake-woman who is associated with
demons, elves, and fairies (I.55-56, 147, 200) and commands
"viewless servants" to work her magic (II.111-141). At the con-

---

[13] In a letter to Woodhouse, 22 September 1819, Keats mentions entering "fully into the feeling" ("in my dramatic capacity") in *Isabella;* he
was wrong in going on to say that "There is no objection of this kind to
Lamia" (*Letters,* II, 174).

[14] Though students sometimes take Lamia's "Why do you think?"
(II.41) as simply "Why do you think I sigh?" (in answer to Lycius' "Why
do you sigh . . . ?" in the preceding line), the question is surely to be
related to the cold philosophy of "think" and "thought" elsewhere in the
poems—e.g., *Endymion,* IV.303-305 ("Alas, I must not think . . ."); *Ode
to a Nightingale,* l. 27 ("Where but to think is to be full of sorrow"); *Ode
on a Grecian Urn,* l. 44 ("tease us out of thought")—and to Keats's "O
for a Life of Sensations rather than of Thoughts!" in the letter to Benjamin Bailey of 22 November 1817 (*Letters,* I, 185).

[15] Evert, pp. 271-275.

clusion Apollonius does what he has to do, and Lamia is revealed to Lycius as a serpent and a "foul dream" (II.271). When he fully faces the reality of the situation Lycius falls dead.

For the same reason that I think Keats placed *Lamia* first among the pieces in the 1820 volume, the poem serves well to introduce the basic Keatsian conflict between mundane reality and some extra-worldly ideal state. The opposition is clearer in this poem than in any other, and it is not resolved, in part because, by the end of the poem, all three of the principal characters are made to seem flawed: Lamia is again a snake-woman, Lycius is a hoodwinked dreamer, and Apollonius is the "cold" philosopher whose manner of realistic perception is, in the narrator's as well as both Lycius' and Lamia's view, rendered similarly unattractive. (The famous passage on "cold philosophy," II.229–238, sets up a number of things as valuable—"an Angel's wings," "mysteries," "the haunted air, and gnomed mine"—that in other poems and even earlier in *Lamia* Keats would be glad to have made "fly"; but here they are in the same category with the rainbow and the "tender-person'd Lamia," and Apollonius momentarily seems to deserve the wreath of "spear-grass and the spiteful thistle" that the narrator awards him, II.228.) The conclusion is quite unsatisfactory, except that, given Lycius' mortal nature, it seems impossible to substitute any other ending as a better one. As a deadlock in the conflict between reality and an ideal, it represents in the 1820 volume a starting point of massive irresolution, which the other narratives and shorter poems that follow, as I have briefly suggested elsewhere, gradually work to clear up and resolve.[16]

III

There are lines in *Lamia* that may be taken as evidence of serious worry on Keats's part, toward the end of his brief career, con-

[16] See "Imagination and Reality in the Odes," below, the final paragraph of section II.

cerning the value of his art.[17] As a symbol of the human investment in a visionary ideal, Lamia rightly deserves exposure: mortal
man cannot live indefinitely in a "purple-lined palace of sweet
sin," cannot entirely forswear "the noisy world," cannot help
"thinking" (II.29–39), because, as Keats wrote in a discarded
passage of Part II, "Spells are but made to break." [18] As a symbol
of poetry itself, however, Lamia presents a more complicated
problem. That the "sole . . . and lone / Supportress of the faery-
roof" of the banquet room is "A haunting music" makes clear
both the association of her magic with poetry and the fragil-
ity of the products of poetic creation—the music "made moan
. . . as fearful the whole charm might fade" (II.122–124). It is
not just angels' wings, mysteries, and the like that "cold philosophy" may cause to fly, but, at this point in the poem, poetry itself. And in expressing this worry—which I do not think is a
primary concern of *Lamia,* a poem that in the over-all view is
surely about life rather than about poetry—Keats is back where
he was in the epistles and other poems of his 1817 volume, pondering the basic worth of poetic art. If the magically produced
banquet room is the most substantial thing that poetry can create,
there are too many Apolloniuses (and not all of them *Blackwood's* and *Quarterly* reviewers) to put it down. This incidental
motif in *Lamia* is, however, an important question in the revision of *Hyperion* that Keats undertook in the same summer
months in which he was writing *Lamia.*

Right from the outset, the revision of the epic fragment, now
called *The Fall of Hyperion,* seems to announce itself as a poem
about dreaming (the new work is subtitled "A Dream"). In the
eighteen-line first paragraph, "dreams" are mentioned five times;
they are identified with "Imagination" and with "visions," and

[17] On this point see, among others, Edward E. Bostetter, *The Romantic
Ventriloquists* (Seattle, 1963), pp. 161–164; and Evert, pp. 275–279.
[18] *The Poetical Works of John Keats,* ed. H. W. Garrod, 2nd ed. (Oxford, 1958), p. 205.

made the substance of "Poesy"; they are also linked with knowledge of "paradise" and "Heaven." And in this opening paragraph
dreaming is set forth as a good activity: the poet is going to "rehearse" a dream, and whether it "Be Poet's or Fanatic's"—i.e.,
whether it succeeds as poetry or puts the poet in the same class
with the inarticulate visionaries, the fanatics and savages of lines
1–4—"will be known / When this warm scribe my hand is in
the grave." In this work, however, after the first half-dozen lines,
dreaming is not to be taken as the kind of large metaphorical
or hypothetical opposite to life in the actual world that it generally is in *Lamia;* in *The Fall of Hyperion* it is more strictly
confined to poetic creation, even to the writing of *The Fall of
Hyperion* itself,[19] and the principal topic, not the claims of the
mortal condition but the value of Keats's own art, is a consid-
erably smaller one than that of the poem just discussed above.

In the introductory narrative, the poet imagines he is in a
garden where he takes a drink of some mysterious juice, falls
into a swoon, and then awakens (in a dream within a dream) to
find himself in a temple, before an altar at the foot of a huge
monument. The priestess Moneta appears and tells him that he
must ascend the steps to the altar or else die. Striving against a
growing numbness, the poet gains the first step:

> One minute before death, my iced foot touch'd
> The lowest stair; and as it touch'd, life seem'd
> To pour in at the toes: I mounted up,
> As once fair Angels on a ladder flew
> From the green turf to heaven.   (I.132–136)

Somewhat like Apollo in *Hyperion,* the poet has died into life:
"Thou has felt," Moneta tells him, "What 'tis to die and live
again before / Thy fated hour" (I.141–143).

At this point follows the dialogue between Moneta and the

---

[19] Irene H. Chayes, "Dreamer, Poet, and Poem in *The Fall of Hyperion,*"
Philological Quarterly, XLVI (1967), 499–515.

poet that has always been the center of interest in the fragment, and has been the focus of a great deal of critical discussion.[20] The poet asks Moneta why he has been allowed up the steps, and she replies:

> None can usurp this height . . .
> But those to whom the miseries of the world
> Are misery, and will not let them rest.
> All else who find a haven in the world,
> Where they may thoughtless sleep away their days,
> If by a chance into this fane they come,
> Rot on the pavement where thou rotted'st half.—
>
> (I.147–153)

The poet remarks that there surely must be thousands "Who feel the giant agony of the world . . . [and] Labour for mortal good" —yet he is "here alone" (I.154–160). Moneta answers,

> They whom thou spak'st of are no vision'ries,
>   . . . they are no dreamers weak,
> They seek no wonder but the human face;
> No music but a happy-noted voice—
> They come not here, they have no thought to come—
> And thou art here, for thou art less than they—
> What benefit canst thou do, or all thy tribe,
> To the great world? Thou art a dreaming thing;
> A fever of thyself—think of the Earth. . . .   (I.161–169)

The lines make a clear-cut distinction between non-poet humanitarians and poet-dreamers, and assert that the latter are "less" than the former. Genuine humanitarians do not come to the temple (clearly the temple of poetry); among poet-dreamers, those who are aware of human misery make it up the steps (achieve fame as poets), and those who are unaware die on the pavement (fail as poets). And Moneta condemns the whole "tribe" of poets.

[20] See the references in Chayes, p. 499 n., and the discussion by Brian Wicker, "The Disputed Lines in *The Fall of Hyperion,*" *Essays in Criticism,* VII (1957), 28–41.

Now, however, the poet pursues the question of the use of poetry—"sure not all / Those melodies sung into the world's ear / Are useless: sure a poet is a sage; / A humanist, Physician to all men" (I.187–190)—and he receives a stinging reply:

> The poet and the dreamer are distinct,
> Diverse, sheer opposite, antipodes.
> The one pours out a balm upon the world,
> The other vexes it.   (I.199–202)

These lines introduce a new distinction into the poem between the true poet, who does good for the world ("pour[ing] . . . balm" is very similar to the recurring notion of the function of poetry in Keats's 1817 volume—e.g., "To sooth the cares, and lift the thoughts of man" in *Sleep and Poetry,* l. 247), and the dreamer, who "vexes" the world (presumably in the same way that imagination "spoils the singing of the Nightingale" in the verse epistle to Reynolds, l. 85).

W. J. Bate has identified two seemingly permanent difficulties in this dialogue.[21] The first has to do with lines 172–176:

> Every sole man hath days of joy and pain,
> Whether his labours be sublime or low—
> The pain alone; the joy alone; distinct:
> Only the dreamer venoms all his days,
> Bearing more woe than all his sins deserve.

As I have pointed out above, Keats in his other writings views pain and pleasure as inseparable in human life,[22] and it is characteristic of the dreamer that he tries (and fails) to fix boundaries between them. Here the situation is exactly reversed. It is possible that in these lines Keats was thinking not theoretically about the

[21] Bate, pp. 598–600.
[22] See n. 12, above.

nature of human life but more realistically about one's ordinary everyday experiences, which do, after all, consist sometimes of pain and sometimes of joy, "distinct." But the passage does have the tone of a significant pronouncement on life and dreaming, and it does stand in conflict with the import of Keats's statements elsewhere.

The other problem concerns the shift or enlargement of categories already mentioned. Lines 147–181 oppose non-poet humanitarians to poet-dreamers, and lines 189–210 distinguish between poets and dreamers; in effect, where Moneta treats all poet-dreamers scornfully in the first half of the dialogue, she praises poets and condemns only dreamers in the second half. It is true that the latter distinction occurs in the so-called "disputed lines" of the poem, but Keats wrote these lines currently in his draft, and presumably had some sense of how they related to the preceding lines.[23] One has to say finally that the minute progress of the argument is not clear, and never will be. In the larger view, how-

[23] In the two transcripts by Woodhouse and his clerk (Garrod's W^2 and T in *The Poetical Works*), the present ll. 187–201½, 205–210 are marked with a penciled line, in the margin in W^2 and vertically through the text in T, and accompanied by a note (initialed by Woodhouse in T), "K. seems to have intended to erase this & the next 21 lines." The fact that the lines were copied currently in the transcripts and the wording of Woodhouse's note (*"seems* to have intended") make virtually certain that the lines were not marked for deletion or revision in Keats's holograph, and that Woodhouse's note is a supposition (most probably based on the duplication of ll. 187, 194–198 in ll. 211, 216–220, but perhaps also on the mix-up of the categories of poet-dreamer, poet, and dreamer in the dialogue). The fact that the present ll. 202½–204 (from "Then shouted I") were added marginally or on a verso page in the transcripts and were not included in Woodhouse's count of "this & the next 21 lines" suggests that Keats later *expanded* the section that Woodhouse thought he "intended to erase." The conclusion is that the lines did exist (pretty much as we now have them) in Keats's holograph, and Woodhouse's note must be treated as a *critical* conjecture rather than a textual fact (Murry, p. 240, says that "I should, myself, have been forced to [Woodhouse's] conclusion if no such statement of Woodhouse's were in existence").

ever, the general drift is unmistakable: Keats wished to establish the categories of non-poet humanist (the highest), humanist
poet (the next best), and dreamer-poet (the lowest), and to af-
firm that there is some use in poetry, even if he is not altogether
sure that (by having mounted up the steps) he himself is a humanist poet.

Following the dialogue, as if to show the poet as humanist,
Keats takes up again the narrative of *Hyperion,* presenting parts
of Book I of the earlier fragment in the form of a vision revealed
to the poet by Moneta. And now, of course, he is right back in
the position he was in when he gave up *Hyperion* in the spring.
He still has on his hands the dead weight of the original composition—the gods at war, the lofty and abstract portrayal of
change, and so on—and is no nearer to making the story humanly
meaningful than he was in the first place. And so he leaves off
again, just as he had before. The poem had "too many Miltonic
inversions in it," he told Reynolds upon giving it up a second
time, two days after he wrote *To Autumn* (*Letters,* II, 167), but
what I think he meant, if he was not just making up an excuse
to hide another reason, is that he had focused too exclusively on
a Milton-like mythology of gods. There are no Adam and Eve
in the parts of *Paradise Lost* that *Hyperion* most closely draws
on, and there are no Adam and Eve in *Hyperion* or *The Fall of
Hyperion* ("our Mother Eve" has already departed, in the latter
work, leaving "refuse of a meal . . . empty shells . . . and rem-
nants more," I.30–33).[24] Moneta had said, "think of the Earth";
but except in incidental details the poetry of earth was still
missing.

IV

The point of all this is to suggest that Keats needed a specific
sort of theme in order to write his best poems, and that this

[24] For a contrary view, see Stuart M. Sperry, Jr., "Keats, Milton, and
The Fall of Hyperion," PMLA, LXXVII (1962), 77–84.

theme had to have something to do with "the heart and nature of Man." It is no accident that I have quoted so many lines from *Lamia* and practically none from *Hyperion* in the first two sections of this essay. Like *Endymion, Lamia* is full of what one now calls "Keatsian" concerns—dreaming, illusion, a mortal-immortal union, the separation of actual and ideal worlds, the impingement of reality, and so on; and also like *Endymion, Lamia* has many passages that relate to and help explain other Keats poems. In *Hyperion* there is virtually nothing of the same sort. Saturn's loss of "My strong identity, my real self" (I.114) and Apollo's "Knowledge enormous" (III.113–120) stand out as significant precisely *because* there are so few of Keats's usual preoccupations in the fragment. There are fine sentiments—for example, "'tis the eternal law / That first in beauty should be first in might" (II.228–229)—but we do not take these as "Keatsian" themes, nor do we find echoes of them in other poems.

I think that *Hyperion* parallels the early attempts in the 1817 volume to write of the chivalric past, and that Keats discovered once again that something besides the "days of old," or of the Titans and Olympians even earlier, was necessary as the subject-matter for "modern" poetry.[25] I do not wish to suggest that Keats was *limited* to writing about the aims of the dreamer and the sharp teeth of the world that we see in poem after poem (in any case, "limitation" in so short a career is out of the question). But it is evident in the work of 1818–19 that his imagination caught fire when it confronted human problems, and went cold when it did not.[26] The completeness of *Lamia* and the fragmentary state

[25] See the first essay in the present volume. *Lamia,* of course, is set "Upon a time, before the faery broods / Drove Nymph and Satyr from the prosperous woods . . ." (I.1–2), but the setting is incidental, and the story is modern. Were it genuinely a poem of the past in the sense of my discussion here, Lycius could have continued indefinitely in his dream, and Apollonius, if he were in the poem at all, would have merely blessed the couple.

[26] Evert, p. 238, points out that when Keats tells his brother and sister-

of the Hyperion poems may serve as illustrations of this simple
fact.

---

in-law, 14 February 1819, that he has "not gone on with *Hyperion*—for to
tell the truth I have not been in great cue for writing lately" (*Letters,* II,
62), he does at the same time promise to send them among other things
The Eve of St. Agnes, which he had just completed. "The inference," says
Evert, "is that he had not been in cue for writing the sort of poem that
Hyperion was intended to be."

⤳§   # The Hoodwinking
of Madeline: Skepticism
in *The Eve of St. Agnes*

I

The commonest response to *The Eve of St. Agnes* has been the celebration of its "heady and perfumed loveliness." The poem has been called "a monody of dreamy richness," "one long sensuous utterance," "an expression of lyrical emotion," "a great affirmation of love," "a great choral hymn," an expression of "unquestioning rapture," and many things else. Remarks like these tend to confirm one's uneasy feeling that what is sometimes called "the most perfect" of Keats's longer poems is a mere fairy-tale romance, unhappily short on meaning. For many readers, as for Douglas Bush, the poem is "no more than a romantic tapestry of unique richness of color"; one is "moved less by the experience of the characters than . . . by the incidental and innumerable beauties of descriptive phrase and rhythm." [1]

To be sure, not all critics have merely praised Keats's pictures. After all, the poem opens on a note of "bitter chill," and pro-

[1] *John Keats: Selected Poems and Letters* (Boston, 1959), pp. xvi, 333; see also Bush's "Keats and His Ideas," in *The Major English Romantic Poets: A Symposium in Reappraisal,* ed. Clarence D. Thorpe et al. (Carbondale, 1957), pp. 239–240. The view is sanctioned by Keats himself, who thought the poem was in some ways like *Isabella*—"too smokeable," with "too much inexperience of . . . [life], and simplicity of knowlege in it," "A weak-sided Poem"; when he later planned a new attempt in poetry, it was "the colouring of St Agnes eve" that he would "diffuse . . . throughout a Poem in which Character and Sentiment would be the figures to such drapery" (*The Letters of John Keats,* ed. Hyder E. Rollins, Cambridge, Mass., 1958, II, 174, 234).

gresses through images of cold and death before the action gets under way. When young Porphyro comes from across the moors to claim his bride, he enters a hostile castle, where Madeline's kinsmen will murder even upon holy days; and in the face of this danger he proceeds to Madeline's bedchamber. With the sexual consummation of their love, a storm comes up, and they must escape the castle, past "sleeping dragons," porter, and blood-hound, out into the night. The ending reverts to the opening notes of bitter chill and death: Madeline's kinsmen are benight-mared, the old Beadsman and Madeline's nurse Angela are gro-tesquely dispatched into the next world. Some obvious contrasts are made in the poem: the lovers' youth and vitality are set against the old age and death associated with Angela and the Beadsman; the warmth and security of Madeline's chamber are contrasted with the coldness and hostility of the rest of the castle and the icy storm outside; the innocence and purity of young love are played off against the sensuousness of the revelers else-where in the castle; and so on. Through these contrasts, says one critic, Keats created a tale of young love "not by forgetting what everyday existence is like, but by using the mean, sordid, and commonplace as a foundation upon which to build a high ro-mance"; the result is no mere fairy tale, but a poem that "has a rounded fulness, a complexity and seriousness, a balance which remove it from the realm of mere magnificent tour de force." [2]

But still something is wanting. The realistic notes all seem to occur in the framework, and the main action is all romance. There is no interaction between the contrasting elements, and hence no conflict. Porphyro is never really felt to be in danger; through much of the poem the lovers are secluded from the rest of the world; and at the end, when they escape, they meet no obstacle, but rather "glide, like phantoms, into the wide hall; / Like phantoms, to the iron porch, they glide. . . . By one, and

<hr>

[2] R. H. Fogle, "A Reading of Keats's 'Eve of St. Agnes,'" *College Eng-lish*, VI (1945), 328, 325.

one, the bolts full easy slide:— / The chains lie silent . . . The key turns . . . the door upon its hinges groans. / And they are gone" (361–370). It is all too easy. Though the poem ends with the nightmares of the warriors, and the deaths of Angela and the Beadsman, the lovers seem untouched, for they have already fled the castle. And besides, this all happened "ages long ago" (370). We are back where we started, with a fairy-tale romance, unhappily short on meaning.

The only serious attempt to make something of the poem has come from a small group of critics whom I shall call "metaphysical critics" because they think Keats was a metaphysician.[3] To them the poem seems to dramatize certain ideas that Keats held a year or two earlier about the nature of the imagination, the relationship between this world and the next, and the progress of an individual's ascent toward spiritualization.

According to the popular superstition connected with St. Agnes' Eve, a young maiden who fasts and neither speaks nor looks about before she goes to bed may get sight of her future husband in a dream. Madeline follows this prescription, dreams of her lover, then seems to awaken out of her dream to find him present in her chamber, an actual, physical fact. Her dream in a sense comes true. The events are thought to relate to a passage in the well-known letter to Benjamin Bailey, 22 November 1817, in which Keats expressed his faith in "the truth of Imagination": "What the imagination seizes as Beauty must be truth—whether it existed before or not. . . . The Imagination may be compared to Adam's dream—he awoke and found it truth." For the meta-

[3] Earl R. Wasserman, *The Finer Tone: Keats' Major Poems* (Baltimore, 1953), pp. 97–137, R. A. Foakes, *The Romantic Assertion* (London, 1958), pp. 85–94, and, at some points, Bernard Blackstone, *The Consecrated Urn* (London, 1959), pp. 275–288, may be included. While Foakes discusses among Keats's poems only *The Eve of St. Agnes,* the metaphysical critics as a group represent not so much an interpretation of the poem as a view of all Keats's poetry. As will appear presently, I think *The Eve of St. Agnes* illuminates a quite different view of Keats's concerns and achievement.

physical critics, just as Adam dreamed of the creation of Eve, then awoke to find his dream a truth—Eve before him a beautiful reality—so Madeline dreams of Porphyro and awakens to find him present and palpably real.

But the imagination is not merely prophetic: it is "a Shadow of reality to come" hereafter; and in the same letter Keats is led on to "another favorite Speculation"—"that we shall enjoy ourselves here after by having what we called happiness on Earth repeated in a finer tone and so repeated. . . . Adam's dream will do here and seems to be a conviction that Imagination and its empyreal reflection is the same as human Life and its spiritual repetition" (*Letters,* I, 184-185). The idea is that a trust in the visionary imagination will allow us to "burst our mortal bars," to "dodge / Conception to the very bourne of heaven," [4] to transcend our earthly confines, guess at heaven, and arrive at some view of the reality to come. If the visionary imagination is valid, the earthly pleasures portrayed in our visions will make up our immortal existence—will be spiritually "repeated in a finer tone and so repeated."

In this sense, Madeline's dream of Porphyro is a case history in the visionary imagination. According to the metaphysical critics, she is, in her dream, at heaven's bourne, already enjoying a kind of spiritual repetition of earthly happiness. On being roused by Porphyro, she finds in him "a painful change" (300): "How chang'd thou art! how pallid, chill, and drear!" she says to him; "Give me that voice again . . . Those looks immortal" (311-313). Porphyro's reply takes the form of action: "Beyond a mortal man impassion'd far / At these voluptuous accents, he arose" (316-317). He transcends his mortal existence, joins Madeline at heaven's bourne by melting into her dream, and together they store up pleasures to be immortally repeated in a finer tone.

The other main strand of the critics' thinking concerns the apotheosis of Porphyro. By relating the poem to Keats's simile

[4] *I stood tip-toe,* l. 190; *Endymion,* I.294-295.

of human life as a "Mansion of Many Apartments," the critics
would persuade us that the castle of Madeline's kinsmen allegori-
cally represents human life, and that Porphyro, passing upward
to a closet adjoining Madeline's bedchamber, and thence into the
chamber itself, progresses from apartment to apartment in the
mansion of life, executing a spiritual ascent to heaven's bourne.
For a number of reasons, Keats's simile confuses rather than
clarifies the poem.[5] But the idea of spiritual pilgrimage is not
entirely to be denied. Porphyro says to the sleeping Madeline,
"Thou art my heaven, and I thine eremite" (277), and when she
awakens, after the consummation, he exclaims to her: "Ah, silver
shrine, here will I take my rest / After so many hours of toil and
quest, / A famish'd pilgrim,—saved by miracle" (337-339).

In brief summary, the main points of the metaphysical critics'
interpretation are that Madeline's awakening to find Porphyro in
her bedroom is a document in the validity of the visionary imagination; that Porphyro in the course of the poem makes a spiritual pilgrimage, ascending higher by stages until he arrives at
transcendent reality in Madeline's bed; and that there the lovers
reenact earthly pleasures that will be stored up for further, still
more elevated repetition in a finer tone. If these ideas seem far-
fetched and confused, the fact should be attributed in part to the
brevity of my exposition, and to the shortcomings of any attempt
to abstract ideas from a complicated poem, even when it is treated

[5] The simile occurs in a letter to J. H. Reynolds, 3 May 1818 (*Letters,*
I, 280–281). Porphyro's eagerness to get to Madeline hardly accords with
Keats's idea that "we care not to hasten" to "the second Chamber"; the
identification of Madeline's bedroom with "the Chamber of Maiden-
Thought" seems similarly unbefitting, since one of the effects of arriving
in the latter is "that tremendous one of sharpening one's vision into the
heart and nature of Man—of convincing ones nerves that the World is full
of Misery and Heartbreak, Pain, Sickness and oppression." Wasserman de-
velops the comparison on pp. 116–125, only to withdraw the letter from
consideration (because "the reading of the romance in the light of the
prose statement suggests an allegorical interpretation") on pp. 131–132;
but he subsequently returns to "the chambers of life" on pp. 159, 164.

as allegory. Yet one may suggest reasons for hesitating to accept them.

For one thing, when the imaginative vision of beauty turns out to be a truth—when Madeline awakens to find Porphyro in her bed—she is not nearly so pleased as Adam was when he awoke and discovered Eve. In fact, truth here is seemingly undesirable: Madeline is frightened out of her wits, and she laments, "No dream, alas! alas! and woe is mine! / Porphyro will leave me here to fade and pine" (328–329). For another, it is a reversal of Keats's own sequence to find in the poem the spiritual repetition of earthly pleasures. In Madeline's dream the imaginative enactment of pleasure comes first; it is an earthly repetition of spiritual pleasure that follows, and perhaps in a grosser, rather than a finer, tone. That the lovers are consciously intent on experiencing the conditions of immortality—consciously practicing for the spiritual repetition of pleasure at an even higher level of intensity—implies, if one reads the critics correctly, that both Madeline and Porphyro have read *Endymion,* Keats's letters, and the explications of the metaphysical critics.[6]

Much of the critics' interpretation rests on the religious language of the poem. Madeline is "St. Agnes' charmed maid," "a mission'd spirit" (192–193), "all akin / To spirits of the air" (201–202), "a saint," "a splendid angel, newly drest, / Save wings, for heaven," "so pure a thing, so free from mortal taint" (222–225). To Porphyro, her "eremite," she is "heaven" (277), and from closet to bedchamber he progresses from purgatory to paradise. Finally, Porphyro is "A famish'd pilgrim,—saved by miracle" (339). But the significance of such language is questionable.

---

[6] So the critics sometimes write: e.g., "Porphyro has recognized that the dream-vision for which Madeline is preparing is an ascent to the 'chief intensity,' to the spiritual repetition of what we call happiness on earth; and therefore the feast and the music represent the sensuous and imaginative entrances into essence before the spiritual entrance through love. Consequently, when Porphyro passes into Madeline's chamber he first prepares the remarkably rich foods . . ." (Wasserman, p. 114).

In *Romeo and Juliet,* with which *The Eve of St. Agnes* has much in common, Juliet's hand at the first meeting of the lovers is a "holy shrine," and Romeo's lips are "two blushing pilgrims"; subsequently Juliet is a "dear saint," a "bright angel," a "fair saint"; "heaven is . . . Where Juliet lives," and outside Verona is "purgatory, torture, hell itself"; she is compared to a "winged messenger of heaven," and her lips carry "immortal blessing." At the same time Romeo is "the god of [Juliet's] idolatry," and a "mortal paradise of . . . sweet flesh."[7] In other poems Keats himself, in the manner of hundreds of poets before him, uses religious terms in hyperbolic love language: for example, Isabella's lover Lorenzo is called "a young palmer in Love's eye," he is said to "shrive" his passion, and (in a stanza ultimately rejected from the poem) he declares that he would be "full deified" by the gift of a love token.[8]

What is perhaps most telling against the critics, in connection with the religious language of *The Eve of St. Agnes,* is that when Porphyro calls himself "A famish'd pilgrim,—saved by miracle," his words must be taken ironically, unless Keats has forgotten, or hopes the reader has forgotten, all the action leading to the consummation. The miracle on which Porphyro congratulates himself is in fact a *stratagem* that he has planned and carried out to perfection. Early in the poem, when he first encounters Angela, she is amazed to see him, and says that he "must hold water in a witch's sieve, / And be liege-lord of all the Elves and Fays, / To venture" into a castle of enemies (120–122). Although Porphyro later assures Madeline that he is "no rude infidel" (342), the images in Angela's speech tend to link him with witches and fairies rather than with the Christian pilgrim. By taking a closer look at the poem, we may see that Keats had misgivings about

[7] I.v.96–97, 105; II.ii.26, 55, 61; III.iii.29–30, 18; II.ii.28; III.iii.37; II.ii.114; III.ii.82.

[8] Lines 2, 64, and the rejected stanza following l. 56 (*The Poetical Works of John Keats,* ed. H. W. Garrod, 2nd ed., Oxford, 1958, p. 217).

Porphyro's fitness to perform a spiritual pilgrimage and arrive at heaven.

II

Porphyro's first request of Angela, "Now tell me where is Madeline" (114), is followed by an oath upon the holy loom used to weave St. Agnes' wool, and it is implied that he is well aware what night it is. "St. Agnes' Eve," says Angela, "God's help! my lady fair the conjuror plays / This very night: good angels her deceive!" (123–125). While she laughs at Madeline's folly, Porphyro gazes on her, until "Sudden a thought came like a full-blown rose. . . . then doth he propose / A stratagem" (136–139). The full force of "stratagem" comes to be felt in the poem—a ruse, an artifice, a trick for deceiving. For Angela, the deception of Madeline by good angels is funny; but Porphyro's is another kind of deception, and no laughing matter. She is startled, and calls him "cruel," "impious," "wicked" (140, 143); the harshness of the last line of her speech emphasizes her reaction: "Thou canst not surely be the same that thou didst seem" (144).

Porphyro swears "by all saints" not to harm Madeline: "O may I ne'er find grace / When my weak voice shall whisper its last prayer, / If one of her soft ringlets I displace" (145–148). He next enforces his promise with a suicidal threat: Angela must believe him, or he "will . . . Awake, with horrid shout" his foemen, "And beard them" (151–153). Because Angela is "A poor, weak, palsy-stricken, churchyard thing" (155), she presently accedes, promising to do whatever Porphyro wishes—

> Which was, to lead him, in close secrecy,
> Even to Madeline's chamber, and there hide
> Him in a closet, of such privacy
> That he might see her beauty unespied,
> And win perhaps that night a peerless bride,
> While legion'd fairies pac'd the coverlet,
> And pale enchantment held her sleepy-eyed. (163–169)

At this point our disbelief must be suspended if we are to read the poem as an affirmation of romantic love. We must leave our world behind, where stratagems like Porphyro's are frowned on, sometimes punished in the criminal courts, and enter an imaginary world where "in sooth such things have been" (81). But the narrator's summary comment on the stratagem is that "Never on such a night have lovers met, / Since Merlin paid his Demon all the monstrous debt" (170–171). The allusion is puzzling. Commentators feel that the "monstrous debt" is Merlin's debt to his demon-father for his own life, and that he paid it by committing evil deeds, or perhaps specifically by effecting his own imprisonment and death through the misworking of a spell.[9] However it is explained, it strengthens rather than dispels our suspicion, like Angela's, that Porphyro is up to no good; and, with the earlier images of "legion'd fairies" and "pale enchantment," it brings further associations of fairy lore and sorcery to bear on his actions. Then Angela asserts a kind of orthodox middle-class morality: "Ah! thou must needs the lady wed" (179).

She now leads Porphyro to Madeline's chamber, "silken, hush'd, and chaste," where he takes "covert" (187–188). In the first draft stanza XXI is incomplete, but two versions that can be pieced together call Porphyro's hiding place "A purgatory sweet to view loves own domain" and "A purgatory sweet to what may he attain."[10] The rejected lines, mentioning "purgatory sweet" as a stage toward the "paradise" (244) of Madeline's chamber, are documents in Porphyro's spiritual pilgrimage, perhaps. The ideas of viewing love's own domain, or what he may attain, are documents in the peeping-Tomism that occupies the next few stanzas. As Angela is feeling her way toward the stair, she is met by Madeline, who turns back to help her down to "a safe level

---

[9] See, among others, H. Buxton Forman, ed., *The Poetical Works and Other Writings of John Keats* (London, 1889), II, 84 n.; Roy P. Basler, *Explicator*, III (1944), item 1.

[10] *Poetical Works*, ed. Garrod, p. 244.

matting" (196). If the action is significant, its meaning lies in
the juxtaposition of Madeline's unselfish act of "pious care" (194)
with the leering overtones just before of Porphyro's having hidden himself in her closet, "pleas'd amain" (188) by the success
of his stratagem, and with the tone of the narrator's words immediately following: "Now prepare, / Young Porphyro, for gazing on that bed; / She comes, she comes again, like ring-dove
fray'd and fled" (196–198).

The mention of "ring-dove" is interesting. Porphyro has taken
"covert"—the position of the hunter (or perhaps merely the bird-
watcher). There follows a series of bird images that perhaps may
be thought of in terms of the hunter's game. In a variant to the
stanza Madeline is "an affrighted Swan"; here she is a "ring-
dove"; in the next stanza her heart is "a tongueless nightingale"
(206); later in the poem she is "A dove forlorn" (333); still later
Porphyro speaks of robbing her nest (340), and in a variant says,
"Soft Nightingale, I'll keep thee in a cage / To sing to me." [11]
It is unlikely that all these images carry connotations of hunting,
nest-robbing, and caging; Romeo will "climb a bird's nest" when
he ascends the ladder to Juliet's room (II.v.76). But the single
comparison of Madeline's heart to a "tongueless nightingale"
seems significant. Leigh Hunt naturally missed the point: "The
nightingale! how touching the simile! the heart a 'tongueless
nightingale,' dying in that dell of the bosom. What thorough
sweetness, and perfection of lovely imagery!" [12] Critics pointing
to Sotheby's translation of Wieland's *Oberon* (VI.17), or to
Troilus and Criseyde (III.1233–39), may also have missed the
significance.[13] For Keats's image embraces the entire story of the
rape of Philomel, and with it he introduces a further note of

[11] For the variants see *Poetical Works,* ed. Garrod, pp. 245, 253.

[12] *Leigh Hunt's London Journal,* II (1835), 18.

[13] Sidney Colvin, *John Keats: His Life and Poetry* . . . (New York,
1925), p. 87 n.; F. E. Priestley, "Keats and Chaucer," *Modern Language Quarterly,* V (1944), 444.

evil that prevents us from losing ourselves in the special morality of fairy romance. Madeline has the status of one of St. Agnes' "lambs unshorn" (71); she is a maiden innocent and pure, but also is about to lose that status through what is in some ways a cruel deception. The comparison with Philomel is not inappropriate.

In stanza XXV, as Madeline is described kneeling, we are told that "Porphyro grew faint: / She knelt, so pure a thing, so free from mortal taint" (224–225). Though many reasons will suggest themselves why Porphyro grows faint, a novel one may be offered here. In his copy of *The Anatomy of Melancholy,* after a passage in which Burton tells how "The Barbarians stand in awe of a fair woman, and at a beautiful aspect, a fierce spirit is pacified," Keats wrote: "abash'd the devil stood." [14] He quotes from Book IV of *Paradise Lost,* where Satan is confronted by the beautiful angel Zephon: "Abasht the Devil stood, / And felt how awful goodness is, and saw / Virtue in her shape how lovely, saw, and pin'd / His loss" (846–849). But since Burton speaks of standing "in awe of a fair woman," Keats must also have recalled Book IX, in which Satan's malice is momentarily overawed by Eve's graceful innocence: "That space the Evil one abstracted stood / From his own evil, and for the time remain'd / Stupidly good" (463–465). Porphyro's faintness may in some way parallel Satan's moment of stupid goodness. "But the hot Hell that always in him burns" soon ends Satan's relapse from evil intent, as he goes about Eve's ruin. So with Porphyro; for "Anon his heart revives" (226), as he pursues the working-out of his stratagem.

Madeline undresses, then falls fast asleep. Porphyro creeps to the bed, "Noiseless as fear in a wide wilderness" (250), and " 'tween the curtains peep'd, where, lo!—how fast she slept" (252). At the bedside he sets a table, when, in the midst of his

[14] *The Poetical Works and Other Writings of John Keats,* ed. H. B. and M. B. Forman (New York, 1938–39), V, 310. (This edition is hereafter cited as "Hampstead Keats.")

preparations, a hall door opens in the castle, and the revelers'
music shatters the silence of the room. Porphyro calls for a
"drowsy Morphean amulet" (257)—and then "The hall door
shuts . . . and all the noise is gone" (261). Madeline continues
sleeping, while he brings from the closet the feast of candied
apple, quince, plum, and all the rest.

Aside from the unheroic implications of "Noiseless as fear in
a wide wilderness" and of the word "peep'd," there are three
things worth noting in the stanzas just summarized. One is the
relationship the poem has here with *Cymbeline,* II.ii.11–50, in
which the villainous Iachimo emerges from the trunk, where he
has hidden himself, to gaze on the sleeping Imogen. Readers since
Swinburne have noted resemblances.[15] Imogen is "a heavenly
angel," and like Madeline a "fresh lily," "whiter than the sheets,"
as she lies in bed, sleeping, in effect, an "azure-lidded sleep"
(262)—and so on. But no critic has been willing to include
among the resemblances that Porphyro's counterpart in the scene
is a villain. In the speech from which these details have been
drawn, Iachimo compares himself with Tarquin, who raped
Lucrece, and he notes that Imogen "hath been reading late / The
tale of Tereus; here the leaf's turn'd down / Where Philomel
gave up."

The second point concerns Porphyro's call for a "drowsy
Morphean amulet"—a sleep-inducing charm to prevent Madeline's awakening when the music bursts forth into the room.
Earlier he has wished to win Madeline while "pale enchantment
held her sleepy-eyed" (169). Here he would assist "pale enchantment" with a "Morphean amulet." It may not be amiss to recall
Lovelace, and the stratagem by which he robbed Clarissa of her
maidenhood. "I know thou wilt blame me for having had re-

---

[15] See Thomas B. Stroup, "Cymbeline, II, ii, and The Eve of St. Agnes,"
English Studies, XVII (1935), 144–145; Claude Lee Finney, *The Evolution
of Keats's Poetry* (Cambridge, Mass., 1936), II, 557–558; *Times Literary
Supplement,* 6 April, 4 May, 1 June 1946, pp. 163, 211, 259.

course to *Art*," writes Lovelace to John Belford, in Richardson's novel. "But do not physicians prescribe opiates in acute cases." Besides, "a Rape, thou knowest, to us Rakes, is far from being an undesirable thing." [16]

The third point has to do with the feast that Porphyro sets out. In his copy of *The Anatomy of Melancholy,* opposite a passage in which Burton commends fasting as an excellent means of preparation for devotion, "by which chast thoughts are ingendred . . . concupiscence is restrained, vicious . . . lusts and humours are expelled," Keats recorded his approval in the marginal comment "good." [17] It is for some reason of this sort that Madeline fasts, going "supperless to bed" (51). Porphyro's feast seems intended to produce the opposite results, and there is more than a suggestion of pagan sensuality in the strange affair of eastern luxuries that he heaps as if by magic—"with glowing hand" (271)—on the table by the bed.[18]

Next Porphyro tries to awaken Madeline, or so it seems: "And now, my love, my seraph fair, awake! / Thou art my heaven, and I thine eremite" (276–277). The last line carries the suggestion that Porphyro has been reading of the martyrdom, not of St. Agnes, but of Donne's lovers in *The Canonization,* whose bodies are by "reverend love" made "one anothers hermitage." It is curious that in the proposition that follows, "Open thine eyes . . . Or I shall drowse beside thee" (278–279), Porphyro does not wait for an answer: "Thus whispering, his warm, unnerved arm / Sank in her pillow" (280–281). "Awakening up" (289), he takes Madeline's lute and plays an ancient ditty, which causes her to utter a soft moan. It would seem that she does at this point wake up: "Suddenly / Her blue affrayed eyes wide open

[16] *Clarissa,* Shakespeare Head ed. (Oxford, 1930), V, 339–340.

[17] Hampstead Keats, V, 318.

[18] Foakes, p. 91 n., relates the feast to "Paynims" in l. 241, but says that "such suggestions are discontinued as Porphyro is transformed" by kneeling by the bed (297, 305–306) and by being "saved" through the completion of a spiritual journey (337–339).

shone. . . . Her eyes were open, but she still beheld, / Now wide awake, the vision of her sleep" (295–299). Not unreasonably, we might think, she weeps, sighs, and "moan[s] forth witless words" (303).

We shall see in a moment, however, that she has not after all awakened from her trance. The "painful change" she witnesses—the substitution of the genuine Porphyro for the immortal looks and voice of her vision—"*nigh* expell'd / The blisses of her dream" (300–301), came near expelling them, but did not in fact do so. Apparently she is to be thought of as still in her trance, but capable of speaking to the Porphyro before her, when she says, "Ah, Porphyro! . . . but even now / Thy voice was at sweet tremble in mine ear" (307–308). To her request for "that voice again . . . Those looks immortal" (312–313), Porphyro offers neither, but rather impassioned action of god-like intensity. At the end of stanza XXXVI, the image of "St. Agnes' moon" combines the notions of St. Agnes, the patron saint of maidenhood, and Cynthia, the goddess of chastity, and the symbolic combination has "set," gone out of the picture to be replaced by a storm: "meantime the frost-wind blows / Like Love's alarum pattering the sharp sleet / Against the window-panes; St. Agnes' moon hath set" (322–324).

Keats's final manuscript version of the consummation, rejected by his publishers on moral grounds, as making the poem unfit to be read by young ladies, is more graphic. For a rather lame conclusion to Madeline's speech (314–315), he substituted the lines, "See, while she speaks his arms encroaching slow, / Have zoned her, heart to heart,—loud, loud the dark winds blow!" Then he rewrote stanza XXXVI:

> For on the midnight came a tempest fell;
> More sooth, for that his quick rejoinder flows
> Into her burning ear: and still the spell
> Unbroken guards her in serene repose.
> With her wild dream he mingled, as a rose

Marrieth its odour to a violet.
Still, still she dreams, louder the frost wind blows,
Like Love's alarum pattering the sharp sleet
Against the window panes:—St Agnes' Moon hath set.[19]

The revised version makes clearer that Madeline is still dreaming: "still the spell / Unbroken guards her in serene repose." And it makes clearer the connection between the sexual consummation, the setting of St. Agnes' moon, and the rising of the storm. When Porphyro's "quick rejoinder flows / Into her burning ear" ("close rejoinder" in the *E* transcript), we may or may not recall Satan "Squat like a Toad, close at the ear of *Eve*" (IV.800); but one would go out of his way to avoid a parallel between the advent of the storm in Keats's poem and the change in Nature that comes about when our first mother in an evil hour reached forth and ate the fruit: "Earth felt the wound, and Nature from her seat / Sighing through all her Works gave signs of woe, / That all was lost" (IX.782–784). Unlike Eve, however, rather more like Clarissa, Madeline by this time has no choice; the revision heightens the contrast between her innocent unconsciousness and the storm raging outside: "Still, still she dreams, louder the frost wind blows."

As printed, the poem continues: " 'Tis dark: quick pattereth the flaw-blown sleet." Then Porphyro: "This is no dream, my

[19] I quote the revised stanza from the second Woodhouse transcript (*W*² in Garrod's *Poetical Works*). After hearing the new version, Woodhouse wrote to the publisher John Taylor, 19 September 1819, "I do apprehend it will render the poem unfit for ladies, & indeed scarcely to be mentioned to them among the 'things that are.'" Taylor replied six days later that if Keats "will not so far concede to my Wishes as to leave the passage as it originally stood, I must be content to admire his Poems with some other Imprint" (*Letters*, II, 163, 183). According to Woodhouse's note heading one of the transcripts of the poem, Keats "left it to his Publishers to adopt which [alterations] they pleased, & to revise the Whole" (*W*²). See Appendix II, below, for an argument urging that a new text be made, embodying revisions found in the late fair copy (Garrod's *E*) and those noticed as alterations (*w*) in the second Woodhouse transcript (*W*²).

bride, my Madeline!" Another line describes the storm: " 'Tis dark: the iced gusts still rave and beat" (325–327). And now Madeline finally does wake up, if she ever does. Her speech shows a mixed attitude toward what has happened, but above all it is the lament of the seduced maiden: "No dream, alas! alas! and woe is mine! / Porphyro will leave me here to fade and pine.— / Cruel! what traitor could thee hither bring?" (328–330). She will curse not, for her heart is lost in his, or, perhaps more accurately, still lost in her romantic idealization of him. But she is aware that her condition is woeful: Porphyro is cruel; Angela is a traitor; and Madeline is a "deceived thing;— / A dove forlorn and lost" (333). In subsequent stanzas Porphyro soothes her fears, again calls her his bride, and seems to make all wrongs right. He tells her that the storm outside is really only "an elfin-storm from faery land" (343), and that she should "Awake! arise! . . . and fearless be, / For o'er the southern moors I have a home for thee" (350–351). They hurry out of the chamber, down the wide stairs, through the castle door—"And they are gone . . . fled away into the storm" (370–371).

III

After giving so much space to Porphyro, in admittedly exaggerated fashion portraying him as peeping Tom and villainous seducer, I must now confess that I do not think his stratagem is the main concern of the poem. I have presented him as villain in order to suggest, in the first place, that he is not, after all, making a spiritual pilgrimage, unless the poem is to be read as a satire on spiritual pilgrimages; in the second place, that the lovers, far from being a single element in the poem, are as much protagonist and antagonist as Belinda and the Baron, or Clarissa and Lovelace; and in the third place, that no matter how much Keats entered into the feelings of his characters, he could not lose touch with the claims and responsibilities of the world he lived in.

Certainly he partially identified himself with Porphyro. When

Woodhouse found his revisions objectionable, Keats replied that he should "despise a man who would be such an eunuch in sentiment as to leave a maid, with that Character about her, in such a situation: & sho^d despise himself to write about it" (*Letters,* II, 163). One may cite the narrator's obvious relish in Porphyro's situation as Madeline is about to undress—"Now prepare, / Young Porphyro, for gazing on that bed" (196–197)—and Keats's later objection to the poem that "in my dramatic capacity I enter fully into the feeling: but in Propria Persona I should be apt to quiz it myself" (*Letters,* II, 174). But sexual passion worried him: to Bailey he confessed in July 1818, "When I am among Women I have evil thoughts" (I, 341), and he wrote in his copy of *The Anatomy of Melancholy,* "there is nothing disgraces me in my own eyes so much as being one of a race of eyes nose and mouth beings in a planet call'd the earth who . . . have always mingled goatish winnyish lustful love with the abstract adoration of the deity."[20] Though it has touches of humor,[21] *The Eve of St. Agnes* is a serious poem; regardless of the extent to which Keats identified with his hero, he introduced enough overtones of evil to make Porphyro's actions wrong within the structure of the poem.

From now on, however, it may be best to think of Porphyro as representing, like the storm that comes up simultaneously with his conquest, the ordinary cruelties of life in the world. Like Melville, Keats saw

> Too far into the sea; where every maw
> The greater on the less feeds evermore. . . .

[20] Hampstead Keats, V, 309.

[21] E.g., the lame and anticlimactic justification, "in sooth such things have been," as Porphyro's imagination expands from "sight of Madeline, / But for one moment" to the progression "speak, kneel, touch, kiss" (78–81); the picture of Porphyro gazing on Angela "Like puzzled urchin" (129); and some of Porphyro's reactions, relayed with tongue in cheek by the narrator: "The lover's endless minutes slowly pass'd" (182), "lo!— how fast she slept" (252), "It seem'd he never, never could redeem / From such a stedfast spell his lady's eyes" (286–287).

Still do I that most fierce destruction see,
The shark at savage prey—the hawk at pounce,
The gentle Robin, like a pard or ounce,
Ravening a worm.   (*Letters*, I, 262)

Let Porphyro represent one of the sharks under the surface. And
to borrow another figure from Melville, let the main concern of
the poem be the young Platonist dreaming at the masthead: one
false step, his identity comes back in horror, and with a half-
throttled shriek he drops through transparent air into the sea,
no more to rise for ever. There are reasons why we ought not
entirely to sympathize with Madeline. She is a victim of deception, to be sure, but of deception not so much by Porphyro as
by herself and the superstition she trusts in. Madeline the self-
hoodwinked dreamer is, I think, the main concern of the poem,
and I shall spend some time documenting this notion and relating it to Keats's other important poems—all of which, in a sense,
are about dreaming.

   If we recall Keats's agnosticism, his sonnet *Written in Disgust
of Vulgar Superstition* (Christianity), and his abuse in a spring
1819 journal letter of "the pious frauds of Religion" (*Letters*, II,
80), we may be prepared to see a hoodwinked dreamer in the
poem even before we meet Madeline. He is the old Beadsman,
so engrossed in an ascetic ritual that he is sealed off from the
joys of life. After saying his prayers, he turns first through a door
leading to the noisy revelry upstairs. "But no. . . . The joys of
all his life were said and sung: / His was a harsh penance on
St. Agnes' Eve" (22-24). And so he goes another way, to sit
among rough ashes, while the focus of the narrative proceeds
through the door he first opened, and on into the assembly of
revelers, where we are introduced to Madeline and the ritual she
is intent on following. In the final manuscript version, between
stanzas VI and VII, Keats inserted an additional stanza on the
ritual, in part to explain the feast that Porphyro sets out:

'Twas said her future lord would there appear
Offering, as sacrifice—all in the dream—
Delicious food, even to her lips brought near,
Viands, and wine, and fruit, and sugar'd cream,
To touch her palate with the fine extreme
Of relish: then soft music heard, and then
More pleasures follow'd in a dizzy stream
Palpable almost: then to wake again
Warm in the virgin morn, no weeping Magdalen.[22]

Then the poem, as it was printed, continues describing Madeline, who scarcely hears the music, and, with eyes fixed on the floor, pays no attention to anyone around her.

Several things deserve notice. By brooding "all that wintry day, / On love, and wing'd St. Agnes' saintly care" (43–44), and by setting herself apart from the revelers, Madeline presents an obvious parallel with the Beadsman. Both are concerned with prayer and an ascetic ritual; both are isolated from the crowd and from actuality. A second point is that the superstition is clearly an old wives' tale: Madeline follows the prescription that "she had heard old dames full many times declare" (45). It is called by the narrator a "whim": "Full of this whim was thoughtful Madeline" (55). The irony of the added stanza enforces the point. Madeline's pleasures turn out to be palpable in fact. When she awakens to find herself with Porphyro, she is anything but warm: rather, she wakes up to "flaw-blown sleet" and "iced gusts" (325, 327); it is no virgin morn for her; and she is a "weeping Magdalen," who cries, "alas! alas! and woe is mine!" (328). But here, early in the poem, "she saw not: her heart was otherwise: / She sigh'd for Agnes' dreams, the sweetest of the year" (62–63). Perfunctorily dancing along, she is said to be "Hoodwink'd with

[22] This is the version recorded in the W^2 transcript. In Ben Jonson's quatrain, quoted by Hunt from Brand's *Popular Antiquities* and often cited in notes to Keats's poem, the assurance that the ritual produces "an *empty* dream" is worth recalling (*Leigh Hunt's London Journal*, II, 1835, 17).

faery fancy; all amort, / Save to St. Agnes and her lambs unshorn" (70–71).

The superstition is next mentioned when Angela tells that
Madeline "the conjuror plays / This very night: good angels her
deceive!" (124–125). Porphyro thinks of the ritual in terms of
"enchantments cold" and "legends old" (134–135). Proceeding to
her chamber, Madeline is called "St. Agnes' charmed maid," "a
mission'd spirit, unaware" (192–193). When she undresses, "Half-
hidden, like a mermaid in sea-weed" (231), she is perhaps linked
briefly with the drowning Ophelia, whose spreading clothes
momentarily support her "mermaid-like" upon the water; like
Ophelia, she is engrossed in a fanciful dream-world.[23] "Pensive
awhile she dreams awake, and sees, / In fancy, fair St. Agnes in
her bed, / But dares not look behind, or all the charm is fled"
(232–234). This last line carries a double meaning: in following
her ritual, Madeline must look neither "behind, nor sideways"
(53); but the real point is that if she did look behind, she would
discover Porphyro, and then "the charm" would be "fled" for a
more immediate reason.

Asleep in bed, Madeline is said to be "Blissfully haven'd both
from joy and pain . . . Blinded alike from sunshine and from
rain, / As though a rose should shut, and be a bud again" (240–
243). Her dream is "a midnight charm / Impossible to melt as
iced stream," "a stedfast spell" (282–283, 287). It is while she is
in this state of stuporous insensibility—while "still the spell /
Unbroken guards her in serene repose," "Still, still she dreams,
louder the frost wind blows"—that Porphyro makes love to her.
On awakening to learn, "No dream, alas! alas! and woe is mine,"
she calls herself "a deceived thing," echoing Angela's words earlier, "good angels her deceive!" Her condition is pitiful, yet at
the same time reprehensible. Her conjuring (perhaps like Merlin's) has backfired upon her, and as hoodwinked dreamer she

[23] *Hamlet,* IV.vii.176–179. The point is made by Stuart M. Sperry, Jr.,
"Madeline and Ophelia," *Notes and Queries,* new ser., IV (1957), 29–30.

now gets her reward in coming to face reality a little too late. The rose cannot shut, and be a bud again.

IV

Whether *The Eve of St. Agnes* is a good poem depends in large part on the reader's willingness to find in it a consistency and unity that may not in fact be there.[24] But however it is evaluated, it stands significantly at the beginning of Keats's single great creative year, 1819, and it introduces a preoccupation of all the major poems of this year: that an individual ought not to lose touch with the realities of this world.

[24] Keats's conclusion seems a matter for unending debate. The metaphysical critics, remarking that the storm is "an elfin-storm from faery land" and that the lovers "glide, like phantoms" out of the castle, uniformly agree that Madeline and Porphyro transcend mortality, entering an otherworld of eternal felicity, while Angela, the Beadsman, and the warriors remain to die or writhe benightmared. But the "elfin-storm" is Porphyro's explanation; the narrator calls it "a tempest fell" of "frost-wind" and "sharp sleet," and other critics (e.g., Amy Lowell, *John Keats,* Boston, 1925, II, 175; Herbert G. Wright, "Has Keats's 'Eve of St Agnes' a Tragic Ending?" *Modern Language Review,* XL, 1945, 90–94; Bernice Slote, *Keats and the Dramatic Principle,* Lincoln, 1958, pp. 35–36) have suggested that the lovers face reality, perhaps even perish, in the storm. Still another view (Wright, p. 92) is that the lovers face penance in "that second circle of sad hell," the circle of carnal sinners in the fifth canto of the *Inferno,* in which (as Keats described it in his sonnet *On a Dream*) lovers are buffeted about in a storm very much like the one in *The Eve of St. Agnes.* It is possible that Porphyro is evil only to the extent that Madeline is a hoodwinked dreamer, that when she awakens from her dream the evil represented by him is correspondingly reduced, and a happy human conclusion is justified. But it seems doubtful, and one may at this point have to fall back on the remark of the publisher J. A. Hessey, "[Keats] is such a man of fits and starts he is not much to be depended on" (Edmund Blunden, *Keats's Publisher,* London, 1936, p. 56), or that of Haydon, "never for two days did he know his own intentions" (*The Diary of Benjamin Robert Haydon,* ed. Willard B. Pope, Cambridge, Mass., 1960, II, 317). Whatever the fate of the lovers, Woodhouse noted that Keats "altered the last 3 lines to leave on the reader a sense of pettish disgust. . . . He says he likes that the poem should leave off with this Change of Sentiment" (*Letters,* II, 162–163).

In the poems of 1819, Keats's most explicit, unequivocal pronouncement on the conditions of human life comes in the *Ode
on Melancholy*. Life in the world, we are told five or six times
in the statements and images of the third stanza, is an affair in
which pleasure and pain are inseparably mixed. There is no pleasure without pain, and, conversely, if pain is sealed off, so also
is pleasure. One accepts life on these terms, or else suffers a kind
of moral and spiritual emptiness amounting to death. The former
is the better choice: he lives most fully "whose strenuous tongue
/ Can burst Joy's grape against his palate fine." The images of
the first stanza—forgetfulness, narcotics, poisons, death—represent
various ways of avoiding pain in life. But they are rejected (the
whole stanza is a series of negatives) because they also exclude
pleasure and reduce life to nothing ("For shade to shade will
come too drowsily, / And drown the wakeful anguish of the
soul"). The equivalent of these anodynes elsewhere in Keats's
poems is dreaming, trusting in the visionary imagination; and,
to cut short further explanation, the dreamer in the works of
1819 is always one who would escape pain, but hopes, wrongly,
to achieve pleasure.

Take Madeline as the first instance. In bed, under the delusion
that she can achieve bliss in her dream, yet wake up in the virgin
morn no weeping Magdalen, she is "Blissfully haven'd both from
joy and pain" (240)—for all practical purposes in the narcotic
state rejected by the *Ode on Melancholy,* experiencing nothing.
Keats reiterates the idea two lines later, "Blinded alike from sunshine and from rain," and the folly of her delusion is represented
by the reversal of natural process, "As though a rose should shut,
and be a bud again" (242–243). As generally in Keats's poems,
dreaming is attended by fairy-tale imagery: under the spell of
"faery fancy," Madeline plays the conjuror, and Porphyro is linked
in several ways with fairy lore, witchcraft, and sorcery, as well as
pagan sensuality. It is possible that Madeline never completely
awakens from her fanciful dream; for she believes Porphyro

when he tells her that the storm is "an elfin-storm from faery land" (343), and she imagines "sleeping dragons all around" (353) when they hurry out of the castle.[25]

The heroine of *The Eve of Saint Mark*, written a week or so after the completion of *The Eve of St. Agnes*, in some ways resembles Madeline. Among the "thousand things" perplexing Bertha in the volume she pores over are "stars of Heaven, and angels' wings, / Martyrs in a fiery blaze, / Azure saints in silver rays" (29–32). Enwrapped in the legend of St. Mark, "dazed with saintly imag'ries" (56), she ignores the life in the village around her, and cuts herself off from reality—a "poor cheated soul" (69), "lost in dizzy maze" [26] and mocked by her own shadow.

The wretched knight-at-arms in *La Belle Dame sans Merci* is similarly a hoodwinked dreamer. La Belle Dame is "a faery's child"; she sings "A faery's song," speaks "in language strange," and takes him to an "elfin grot." When he awakens from his vision he finds himself "On the cold hill's side." But he is still the dupe of his dream, still hoodwinked, because he continues, in a barren landscape, "Alone and palely loitering," hoping for a second meeting with La Belle Dame. And he denies himself participation in the actual world, which, in contrast to his bleak surroundings, is represented as a more fruitful scene, where "The squirrel's granary is full, / And the harvest's done."

In *Lamia*, the hoodwinked dreamer is of course Lycius, who falls in love with the serpent-woman Lamia, in whose veins runs "elfin blood," who lingers by the wayside "fairily," with whom he lives in "sweet sin" in a magical palace with a "faery-roof" (I.147,

---

[25] When I read an earlier version of this paper before the English faculty of the University of Illinois, it was suggested that if Porphyro awakens Madeline to reality, he should be considered an agent of good in Keats's terms. It may be observed, however, (1) that Madeline dreams through the consummation; and (2) that Porphyro does not necessarily represent all aspects of reality, or even one aspect consistently throughout the poem. Contradiction arises mainly from the assumption of allegory.

[26] A variant following l. 68 (*Poetical Works*, ed. Garrod, p. 451).

200; II.31, 123). "She seem'd, at once, some penanced lady elf, / Some demon's mistress, or the demon's self" (I.55–56). What she promises to do for Lycius is what, according to the *Ode on Melancholy,* cannot be done for mortal men: "To unperplex bliss from its neighbour pain; / Define their pettish limits, and estrange / Their points of contact, and swift counterchange." The inseparability of pleasure and pain is for her a "specious chaos"; she will separate them "with sure art" (I.192–196)—or so the blinded Lycius thinks. But "Spells are but made to break," wrote Keats, in a passage subsequently omitted from the text.[27] "A thrill / Of trumpets" reminds Lycius of the claims of the "noisy world almost forsworn" (II.27–33), and he holds a wedding feast, at which "cold philosophy," in the form of his old tutor Apollonius, attends to put "all charms" to flight. The "foul dream" Lamia vanishes under the tutor's piercing eye, and Lycius, too engrossed in his dream to survive, falls dead.

From *Lamia,* we may merely dip into *The Fall of Hyperion* to recall Keats's condemnation of dreamers.[28] They are "vision'ries," "dreamers weak," who seek out wonders, but ignore what is most important, the human face (I.161–163). "Only the dreamer venoms all his days" (I.175), the speaker learns on the steps of Moneta's temple. "The poet and the dreamer are distinct, / Diverse, sheer opposite, antipodes. / The one pours out a balm upon the world, / The other vexes it" (I.199–202).

Keats's mature view of dreamers illuminates perhaps most importantly the two best odes, *On a Grecian Urn* and *To a Nightingale.* In each poem the speaker begins as dreamer, hoodwinked with the idea that he can unperplex bliss from its neighbor pain, that he can find an anodyne to the ills of the flesh by joining the

---

[27] *Poetical Works,* ed. Garrod, p. 205.

[28] I use the term "dip" advisedly. Moneta is speaking more narrowly of *poet*-dreamers, and part of the condemnation occurs in a passage that Woodhouse thought Keats "intended to erase"

timeless life pictured on an urn, or by fading away into the forest with a bird. In each case the result is an awareness that spells are but made to break: the speaker recognizes the falseness of the dream, the shortcomings of the ideal he has created, and he returns to the mortal world. Life on the urn is at first attractive: unheard melodies are sweeter; the lovers will remain young and fair; the trees will never lose their leaves. Yet it is a static situation. Love must be enjoyed, not be stopped forever at a point when enjoyment is just out of reach. The final judgment is that the urn is a "Cold Pastoral," a "friend to man" that, as a work of art, teases him out of thought but offers no possible substitute for life in the actual world.

In the *Ode to a Nightingale,* the speaker would fade away with the bird, and forget "The weariness, the fever, and the fret" of the mortal world, "Where Beauty cannot keep her lustrous eyes, / Or new Love pine at them beyond to-morrow." But when he imaginatively joins the bird in the forest, he immediately longs for the world he has just rejected: "Here there is no light. . . . I cannot see what flowers are at my feet." "In embalmed darkness" he is forced to "guess each sweet" of the transient natural world. As he continues musing, the bird takes on for him the fairy-tale associations that we saw earlier connected with Madeline's dream, La Belle Dame, and Lamia: its immortal voice has charmed "magic casements . . . in faery lands forlorn." The realization that the faery lands are forlorn of human life tolls the dreamer back to his sole self, and he wakes up. The nightingale, symbol of dreams and the visionary imagination, has turned out to be a "deceiving elf." The fancy "cannot cheat so well."

The metaphysical critics are right in asserting Keats's early trust in the imagination. What they sometimes fail to recognize, themselves eager for glimpses of heaven's bourne, and to an extent hoodwinked with their own rather than Keats's metaphysics, is that before Keats wrote more than a handful of poems we would not willingly let die, he in large part changed his mind.[29] Late in January 1818, on sitting down to read *King Lear* once again, he wrote a sonnet bidding goodbye to romance: "Let me not wander in a barren dream." A few days later he called it "A terrible division" when the soul is flown upward and the body "earthward press'd." In March he wrote, "It is a flaw / In happiness to see beyond our bourn," and about the same time he recognized that "Four Seasons"—not just eternal spring, as the visionary might conjure up—"Four Seasons fill the Measure of the year." Similarly "Four Seasons are there in the mind of Man," who "hath his Winter too of pale Misfeature, / Or else he would forget his mortal nature" (*Letters,* I, 215, 221, 262, 243). In July, on his walking trip to Scotland, he wrote:

> Scanty the hour and few the steps beyond the bourn of care,
> Beyond the sweet and bitter world,—beyond it unaware!
> Scanty the hour and few the steps, because a longer stay
> Would bar return, and make a man forget his mortal way:
> O horrible! . . .
> No, no, that horror cannot be, for at the cable's length
> Man feels the gentle anchor pull and gladdens in its strength.
>   (*Lines Written in the Highlands,* ll. 29–40)

It is the gentle anchor of mortality that ties us to the world; man gladdens in its strength. "Fancy," said Keats to Reynolds, "is indeed less than a present palpable reality" (*Letters,* I, 325). It would be a distortion of fact to maintain that he always held this later view, but it is worth noting that even when he and his fancy

[29] Glen O. Allen, "The Fall of Endymion: A Study in Keats's Intellectual Growth," *Keats-Shelley Journal,* VI (1957), 37–57, argues authoritatively that the change occurred during the winter of 1817–18, while Keats was completing and revising *Endymion.* David Perkins, *The Quest for Permanence* (Cambridge, Mass., 1959), p. 220, feels that "the over-all course of [Keats's] development might be partly described as a periodic, though gradually cumulative, loss of confidence in the merely visionary imagination."

could not agree, he declared himself "more at home amongst Men and women," happier reading Chaucer than Ariosto (II, 234).

The dreamer in Keats is ultimately one who turns his back, not merely on the pains of life, but on life altogether; and in the poems of 1819, beginning with *The Eve of St. Agnes,* his dreaming is condemned. If the major concern in these poems is the conflict between actuality and the ideal, the result is not rejection of the actual, but rather a facing-up to it that amounts, in the total view, to affirmation. It is a notable part of Keats's wisdom that he never lost touch with reality, that he reproved his hood-winked dreamers who would shut out the world, that he recognized life as a complexity of pleasure and pain, and laid down a rule for action: achievement of the ripest, fullest experience that one is capable of. These qualities make him a saner if in some ways less romantic poet than his contemporaries, and they should qualify him as the Romantic poet most likely to survive in the modern world.

The Meaning
of "Poor Cheated Soul"
in *The Eve of Saint Mark*

Most modern criticism sees *The Eve of Saint Mark* (written 13–17 February 1819) as a series of vignettes or pictures, hardly more than the setting for a poem that was never written. The only extensive interpretation is that by Walter E. Houghton,[1] whose main points Douglas Bush incorporates into his own excellent general comment on the poem as follows:

The fragment as a whole . . . turns on implicit or explicit contrasts between life and death, past and present, outdoor and indoor scenes, the externals of ordinary life and human dreams and aspirations. . . . Bertha is the pole of two special contrasts. Her fervently religious reading and imagining are set against the quietude of the town and the placid Sabbath piety of its people; and her "homely room," her humble self, and her black dress, against the exotic decorations of her book and screen and the eerie play of light and shadow about her. . . . It has been argued (by Walter Houghton) that—like a heroine of George Eliot—Bertha was dreaming of the glories of martyrdom and sainthood (although that is not the kind of theme we should expect Keats to choose). At least there seem to be serious implications or possibilities; perhaps Keats did not quite know where he was going. . . .[2]

These "serious implications" can be pinned down to the question of why, in line 69, Bertha is a "poor cheated soul." Professor Houghton has suggested that, as a "modern" English girl dream-

[1] "The Meaning of Keats's *Eve of St. Mark*," *ELH*, XIII (1946), 64–78.
[2] *John Keats: His Life and Writings* (New York and London, 1966), p. 117.

ing of a martyrdom no longer possible, she is cheated of sainthood. The late Mabel Steele, with characteristic practicality, proposed that she is cheated by the failing light ("all was gloom, / Abroad and in the homely room," 67–68).[3] I would urge a third view, which I think has more support from Keats's images than either of these—that, by ignoring the life in the village outside her room, Bertha is cheating herself of reality.

Consider first the character of this "reality," which perhaps can be displayed most clearly by a comparison with Keats's sonnet of more than two years earlier *Written in Disgust of Vulgar Superstition*. Both poems begin with the tolling of church bells, but there are considerable differences in their attitudes toward churchgoing. The "melancholy round" of bells and the "sermon's horrid sound" in the sonnet are entirely negative; the bells of *The Eve of Saint Mark* are "Twice holy" and the organ is "loud and sweet." The churchgoers of the sonnet are objects of scorn, associated with "gloominess" and "dreadful cares," their minds "closely bound / In some black spell"; those of the later fragment are an attractive group, associated with "clean and fair" city streets, "wholesome drench of April rains," and the promise of spring— and they are described as "staid and pious," "patient folk and slow," who move with "demurest air." Quite plainly the town, the countryside, "the folk," and their activity in *The Eve of Saint Mark*, lines 1–22, are presented as a reality that is unambiguously good. These are the things that Bertha has cut herself off from as she pores "all day long" over the "curious volume" containing the life of St. Mark.

Next consider Keats's description of the book in which Bertha is so absorbed. It is "patch'd and torn," decorated with "golden broideries," and it contains

a thousand things,—
The stars of Heaven, and angels' wings,

---

[3] See Bush's note in *John Keats: Selected Poems and Letters* (Boston, 1959), p. 342.

> Martyrs in a fiery blaze,
> Azure saints in silver rays,
> Aaron's breastplate, and the seven
> Candlesticks John saw in Heaven,
> The winged Lion of Saint Mark,
> And the Covenantal Ark,
> With its many mysteries,
> Cherubim and golden mice.   (29–38)

One need not invoke Keats's comments elsewhere on martyrs ("The most bigotted word ever met with," he exclaimed in a note in Burton's *Anatomy;* "I have been astonished that Men could die Martyrs for religion," he told Fanny Brawne),[4] or the famous passage about "cold philosophy" in *Lamia,* II.229–238 (especially close to the above-quoted lines in specifying that "Philosophy will clip an Angel's wings, / Conquer all mysteries . . ."), which is highly ambiguous in its own context and of doubtful applicability here. There is in lines 29–38 a remarkable progress from the general ("things," "stars," "wings," "Martyrs," "saints") to the particular ("breastplate," "seven / Candlesticks," "winged Lion," "Covenantal Ark") in which the images, even though there is Biblical authority for each, are increasingly reminiscent of the relics carried by Chaucer's Pardoner ("a pilwe-beer . . . Oure Lady veyl . . . a gobet of the seyl / That Seint Peter hadde . . . a croys of latoun ful of stones," etc.—*General Prologue,* ll. 694–699). The final juxtaposition in the paragraph, "Cherubim and golden mice," tends to throw ridicule on the rest. Keats's interest here is in the monstrous and exotic, and parallels for these details enforce the point fifty lines later in the description of Bertha's

> warm angled winter screen,
> On which were many monsters seen,

[4] Robert Gittings, *John Keats: The Living Year* (Cambridge, Mass., 1954), p. 197; *The Letters of John Keats,* ed. Hyder E. Rollins (Cambridge, Mass., 1958), II, 223.

Call'd doves of Siam, Lima mice,
And legless birds of Paradise,
Macaw, and tender Av'davat,
And silken-furr'd Angora cat.   (72–82)

Both passages, alike in their focus on unnatural natural history, stress romantic remoteness from the everyday reality outside Bertha's room.

Bertha's own place in this basic opposition of the poem is made clear by the verbs Keats uses to describe her attachment to the volume. Her eyes are "taken captive" (27); she is "Perplex'd" (29) and "dazed with saintly imag'ries" (56); in one manuscript she is said to be a "Maiden lost in dizzy maze"; [5] her own shadow comes "to mock behind her back" (87). These verbs class her with dreamers and pursuers of ritual in other Keats poems—for example, Madeline in *The Eve of St. Agnes,* who is "Hoodwink'd with faery fancy; all amort, / Save to St. Agnes . . ." (70–71); or the speakers in the odes, who are deeply, though not permanently, committed to the Grecian urn and the nightingale (the one "tease[s] us out of thought," the other is a "deceiving elf" that "cheat[s]"); or Lycius in *Lamia,* who is "shut up in mysteries, / His mind wrapp'd like his mantle" (I.241–242). Like them all, she is "cheated"—a "poor cheated soul."

Keats perhaps further ridicules her attachment in the passage of pseudo-Chaucerian Middle English that he added after line 98. Bertha's volume tells of "swevenis" (dreams) and, among other things,

how a litling child mote be
A saint er its nativitie,
Gif that the modre (God her blesse!)
Kepen in solitarinesse,
And kissen devoute the holy croce.   (103–107)

[5] *The Poetical Works of John Keats,* ed. H. W. Garrod, 2nd ed. (Oxford, 1958), p. 451.

In letters of 21 September 1819, the day after he copied out *The Eve of Saint Mark* for his brother and sister-in-law, Keats twice used the phrase "kepen in solitarinesse" to describe his own situation in being left alone while Charles Brown "has gone a visiting"—possibly to the future mother of Charles Brown, Jr., among others.[6] Keats needed neither medical school nor Brown's frequent sexual adventures to remind him that a woman cannot have "a litling child" if she keeps "in solitarinesse" and kisses only "the holy croce." It is not impossible that this last line carries something of the tone of the conclusion of the *Pardoner's Tale:* "Com forth, sire Hoost . . . And thou shalt kisse the relikes everychon."

Bertha very likely has all the romantic longings that Professor Houghton says she does. But Keats, who wrote the poem, did not share them. From his point of view she is as foolish as all the other dreamers so wrapped up in an impossible ideal that they turn away from life itself. He says as much in calling her a "poor cheated soul."

[6] *Letters,* II, 166, 209. Aileen Ward, *John Keats: The Making of a Poet* (New York, 1963), p. 435, suggests that Keats may have added the Chaucerian passage at this time.

Imagination
and Reality
in the Odes

Keats was twenty-three years old when, in the spring and autumn of 1819, he wrote the five odes that many critics consider his finest achievement. He had begun serious composition little more than three years earlier, had published a first volume, *Poems* (1817), and a long narrative poem, *Endymion* (1818), in the two years preceding, and would publish only one more volume, containing the odes and, as the title page has it, *Lamia, Isabella, The Eve of St. Agnes, and Other Poems* (1820), before his death in 1821 at the age of twenty-five. When it was all over, he had the shortest writing career—a span (not counting juvenile effusions) of four years, from the winter of 1815–16 to the end of 1819—of any of the major poets in English, and without question the rapidest development.

It is a nice job to explain that development. The documents concerning the facts of his early life—the upbringing around a London livery stable, enrollment at John Clarke's academy at Enfield, a few miles north of London, when he was seven, the death of his father and hasty remarriage of his mother when he was eight, the death of his mother when he was fourteen—contain no hint of the poet-to-be. His formal education, first at Clarke's school (1803–11), then as an apprentice to an apothecary-surgeon of Edmonton (1811–15), and finally as a medical student at Guy's Hospital, from which after a year's course he emerged in 1816 with a certificate to practice as an apothecary, was meager by the

99

standards of the time for a man of letters. We know that he read widely, in the Latin and English poets, under Clarke's tutelage and on his own. It is not difficult, especially as we see it dramatized in *Poems* of 1817, to understand his desire to be a poet. But it borders on the impossible, once Keats has embarked on his choice, to account fully for the incredibly fast ripening in his work from the earliest imitative efforts, embarrassing in their lushness and sentimentality, to the richest products of his maturity. One can observe, at any stage in their careers, how a Ben Jonson, a Tennyson, or even a Pope *crafted* his poems. With Keats, just as with Shakespeare, one wants, even while knowing better, to invoke the mystery and magic associated with "genius" to say what lay behind the fusion of serious theme with the perfectly controlled sounds and abundance of striking images that we see in his best writing.

One can, however, describe what Keats's poems are about, and in the description at least partially account for his peculiar excellence. He wrote on most of the standard subjects: nature, poetry, art, love, fame, and death. But in the over-all view, his significant poems center on a single basic problem, the mutability inherent in nature and human life, and openly or in disguise they debate the pros and cons of a single hypothetical solution, transcendence of earthly limitations by means of the visionary imagination. If one were to summarize the career in a sentence, it would be something like this: Keats came to learn that this kind of imagination was a false lure, inadequate to the needs of the problem, and in the end he traded it for the naturalized imagination, embracing experience and process as his own and man's chief good. His honesty in treating the problem and his final opting for the natural world, where all the concrete images of poetry come from and where melodies impinge on "the sensual ear" or not at all, are what, more than anything else, guarantee his place "among the English Poets."

I

What goes up must, in reality, come down. Stock notions of "romanticism" to the contrary, the typical lyric of the English Romantic period has the structure of a literal or metaphorical excursion that can best be represented, in blackboard fashion, by the following diagram:[1]

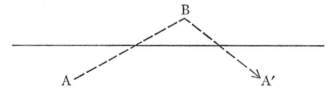

The horizontal line stands for a boundary separating the actual world (below) and the ideal (above). (The two realms have many common labels: earth and heaven, mortality and immortality, time and eternity, materiality and spirituality, the known and the unknown, the finite and the infinite, realism and romance, and so on. The ideal is represented above the line because it is, so to speak, a "higher" reality—what is intended by the difference between "natural" and "*super*natural.") Characteristically, the speaker in a Romantic lyric begins in the real world (A), takes off in mental flight to visit the ideal (B), and then—for a variety of reasons, but most often because he finds something wanting in the imagined ideal or because, being a native of the real world,

[1] Keats himself provides a basis of sorts for this diagram in his second axiom for poetry: "the rise, the progress, the setting of imagery should like the Sun come natural [to the reader] . . . shine over him and set soberly although in magnificence leaving him in the Luxury of twilight" (to John Taylor, 27 February 1818—*The Letters of John Keats,* ed. Hyder E. Rollins, Cambridge, Mass., 1958, I, 238). Northrop Frye might seem to counter the direction of the diagram when he says that "the metaphorical structure of Romantic poetry tends to move inside and downward instead of outside and upward" ("The Drunken Boat: The Revolutionary Element in Romanticism," in *Romanticism Reconsidered,* ed. Frye, New York and London, 1963, p. 16). But his view is not fundamentally incompatible with my description here; he is in effect focusing on the descent from B to A'.

he discovers that he does not or cannot belong permanently in the ideal—returns home to the real (A′). But he has not simply arrived back where he began (hence "A′" rather than "A" at the descent), for he has acquired something—a better understanding of a situation, a change in attitude toward it—from the experience of the flight, and he is never again quite the same person who spoke at the beginning of the poem.

In various ways, hundreds of poems, and not all of them lyrics, may be seen to display this typical structure—to pick examples almost at random, Coleridge's *The Eolian Harp* (mental fantasies leading up to a "what if" speculation about the organic unity of "all of animated nature," followed by a descent to orthodoxy at the end), *The Rime of the Ancient Mariner* (a voyage out to the unknown and subsequent journey home to the real world and society), and poems by Wordsworth as diverse as *A slumber did my spirit seal* (slumber succeeded by awakening, a return of sorts), *Tintern Abbey* (the general progress is from memory to the awareness of "A presence . . . something far more deeply interfused," and then back to memory), the *Intimations* ode (an imaginative excursion to childhood's "visionary gleam" and what it intimates, followed by a return to the adult world of "the light of common day"), all those poems in which a fancied notion is put down by a closer look (e.g., *Resolution and Independence* and *A narrow girdle of rough stones*), and even the Prologue to *Peter Bell,* where a literal flight among the stars proves a terrifying experience for the poet. Many others could be cited, and the structure is of course common to other literatures and art besides those of the early nineteenth century. In *The Wizard of Oz,* Dorothy's "homeward fever" (to borrow a phrase from *Endymion*) is no different from that experienced by a number of cosmically displaced Romantic heroes, and the lesson she learns at the end, "There's no place like home," is a main point, though never in quite such plain language, of some notable poems of Keats's period.

It is not really necessary to place Keats historically—in any sense in which he is "romantic" we are still today in the same "romantic movement"—but it happens that the structure embraces two dominant tendencies in the literature of his time, the desire to transcend the world of flux and the desire to merge with that world, and it helps explain the way in which both of these contradictory tendencies may exist, as they so often do, in the same work. Take Keats's *Bright star* sonnet as a simple case in point: [2]

> Bright star! would I were steadfast as thou art—
>   Not in lone splendour hung aloft the night
> And watching, with eternal lids apart,
>   Like nature's patient, sleepless Eremite,
> The moving waters at their priestlike task
>   Of pure ablution round earth's human shores,
> Or gazing on the new soft fallen mask
>   Of snow upon the mountains and the moors—
> No—yet still steadfast, still unchangeable,
>   Pillow'd upon my fair love's ripening breast,
> To feel for ever its soft fall and swell,
>   Awake for ever in a sweet unrest,
> Still, still to hear her tender-taken breath,
> And so live ever—or else swoon to death.

In terms of the blackboard diagram, the leap from A to B is made in the first line, as the speaker focuses his imagination on a star and its steadfastness. Lines 2–8 explore (and already with "Not" in l. 2 begin to reject) the unearthliness of the star's situation: it shines in *"lone* splendour," is aloof, never sleeps, is associated with a cold and inhuman religious asceticism, and is separated by a considerable distance from the beauties of nature. The sestet makes it clear that the speaker desires this steadfastness not "aloft" but on earth, in his own world of love and movement, "ripening" and "sweet unrest," and that this is the only kind of

[2] In using this example I am specially indebted to David Perkins, *The Quest for Permanence* (Cambridge, Mass., 1959), pp. 231–233.

steadfastness he will settle for ("or else swoon to death"). Thus the speaker has chosen a symbol of unearthly permanence, has stripped away its unearthly qualities, and has concluded by bringing what he wants of the symbol—really the bare notion of steadfastness with which he started—home to the mortal world.

It is a short poem, and the lesson the speaker learns from his imaginative flight—perhaps that the steadfastness of a star is acceptable only with considerable qualification—does not greatly enlarge his understanding (his mind is made up from l. 2 on). But in its preoccupation with time and timelessness, both out of the world and in it, and in its movement of excursion and return, the sonnet epitomizes the principal theme and structure common to the odes. If we ignore (as, in the scope of this essay, I must ignore) most of the subtleties and complexities that make them the great poems that they are, the odes as a group may be read as an investigation of the imagination's ability to cope with time and change: the first three are mainly exploratory, and the final two are written, as it were, with the exploration over and an awareness of the results. And they are all in some degree relatable to the structure I have been discussing: *Nightingale* and *Grecian Urn* follow the pattern of flight and return all the way through, and the others may be thought of as partial exemplifications, centering on the excursion (*Psyche*) or the return (*Melancholy* and *Autumn*).

Ode to Psyche, apparently the earliest of the five odes to be written,[3] is the least clearly organized of the poems and the least

---

[3] Four of the five odes can be dated with a fair degree of certainty. *Psyche* was completed by 30 April 1819 (*Letters*, II, 106–108); *Nightingale* and *Grecian Urn* are both dated May in the transcripts; *To Autumn* was written on 19 September (*Letters*, II, 167). Although *Melancholy* is generally assigned to May, there is actually no evidence for dating it except for its thematic and stylistic similarity to other work of the spring, summer, and autumn of 1819. I should explain that I have omitted *Ode on Indolence,* sometimes classed with the others as the sixth "great ode," on the grounds of its obvious inferiority as a poem (its worth is not much

easy to integrate with the others in any unified view. It is, more than anything else, a poem about mental life in the modern world, and as such it picks up the theme of Keats's dedicatory sonnet *To Leigh Hunt, Esq.* in the 1817 volume, which opens with the statement that "Glory and loveliness have passed away" and goes on to establish the idea—which could serve as one capsule summary of the Romantic movement—that it is up to the poet himself to compensate for the cruel banishment of fairies, gods, myth, and religion by Lockean and Newtonian "cold philosophy." In the ode, the speaker describes Psyche's (and his own) time as an age

> too late for antique vows,
> Too, too late for the fond believing lyre,
> When holy were the haunted forest boughs,
> Holy the air, the water, and the fire   (36–39)

—an age "so far retir'd / From happy pieties" (40–41). In the face of such impoverishment, declaring that he himself will be Psyche's priest, the speaker takes an excursive leap to "some untrodden region of my mind," where he will "build a fane" to worship her (50–51). The poem is the most ambiguous of the odes, and the concluding speculations about the higher reality that the speaker looks forward to can be read in two different ways— either as an affirmation of the successful working of the imagination to re-create lost glory and loveliness (in such a view the imagination would be more akin to Wordsworthian creative sensibility than to the visionary faculty of Keats's other poems), or as a retreat in which the powers of the mind provide only a partial solution. As David Perkins has pointed out,[4] there are various hints of insubstantiality—the "stars without a name" (61), the idea of *feigning* (62), and the questionable delight of "shadowy

enhanced by restoring its stanzas to their proper order: see Appendix IV, especially the final paragraph). Several other "odes" among Keats's poems are also excluded from consideration here.

[4] See Perkins, pp. 226–228.

thought" (65), contrasting strikingly with the luxurious physi-
cality of Cupid's and Psyche's lovemaking in the opening stanza
of the poem—that suggest something less than a triumphant solv-
ing of the problem at the end. It may be that the hypothetical
excursion to "some untrodden region of my mind" leaves the poet
stranded, and at too great a distance from the forest and bedded
grass where he last saw the lovers; whatever the nature of the
perception in the opening stanza—waking dream or "thoughtless" vision (see l. 7)—the "working brain" and "shadowy
thought" of the final lines do not seem an entirely satisfactory
compensation.

Ode to a Nightingale is the first of the odes to bring the speaker
back to reality. In the opening three stanzas, he yearns after an
invisible bird and the condition it symbolizes, an ideal state transcending the mortal world of weariness, fever, and fret, "Where
youth grows pale, and spectre-thin, and dies . . . Where Beauty
cannot keep her lustrous eyes," and so on (23–30). By the middle
of the fourth stanza, he succeeds in joining the bird by means of
imagination, "the viewless wings of Poesy" (33). Almost immediately, however—just as when the "exil'd mortal" Endymion
first discovers himself cut off from familiar surroundings (*Endymion*, II.285–332)—there follows the speaker's vivid realization
of what he has lost by crossing the boundary into an imagined
ideal: "But here [i.e., in the forest] there is no light. . . . I cannot
see what flowers are at my feet," or any of a series of lovingly
detailed images drawn from memory of the transient natural
world that he has left behind and now longs for (38–50). The
rest of the poem represents an ever-widening separation between
speaker and bird. In the sixth stanza, the idea of the richness of
death is nullified by the speaker's abrupt awareness that he would
become a lifeless sod. The seventh stanza, spoken with full knowledge of the difference between mortal speaker and "immortal
Bird," puts the nightingale further and further out of the realm of
ordinary life, associating it with medieval times ("emperor and

clown"), Biblical history ("the sad heart of Ruth," in "alien" surroundings), and finally "faery lands forlorn," where there is no human life at all. In the last stanza, the speaker returns to himself and the real world. The nightingale is suddenly divested of its symbolism as it flies off and the speaker locates it, not in another ideal forest, but in the familiar landscape of "the near meadows . . . the still stream . . . the hill-side . . . the next valley-glades" (76–78). Where before the bird had been "immortal" and the speaker "in embalmed darkness" had longed for death, now the voice of the bird is "buried deep" (77) and the speaker is very much alive. At the end of the poem he is back in the same world from which he took off, but he has learned some significant things in the interim about his own world, his condition in it, and his relationship to the hypothetical ideal symbolized by the bird. The nightingale has proved to be a "deceiving elf," the "fancy" (= imagination) "cheat[s]" (73–74), and he does not seem sorry to return from the final emptiness that he has discovered to be "forlorn.".

In *Ode on a Grecian Urn,* whose movement parallels that of the preceding poem, the hypothetical ideal is the realm of art. The poem offers a beautifully clear example of the way in which meaning results from the structuring of attitudes, for, once the speaker is caught up in the life pictured on the urn (by the end of the first stanza), a seesaw opposition of earthly versus urnly values ensues (11–30) in which, up to a point, the decision could go either way. On the one hand, "Heard melodies are sweet," the piper cannot cease his piping (and may therefore get tired), the trees are confined to a single season, and the lover can never catch or kiss the maiden he is pursuing; on the other hand, "unheard" melodies "Are sweeter," the piper is "unwearied," the boughs are "happy" in their situation, and the lover and the maiden will love and be young and fair forever. The outcome of such an opposition depends of course on the order in which the pros and cons are presented: if B has X quality (good) and Y quality (bad), we can express either an essentially negative attitude ("although B is X, we mustn't overlook Y") or a positive one ("in spite of Y, B is very X") according to our arrangement of the facts. The view of life on the urn is favorable at the end of both the second stanza ("For ever wilt thou love, and she be fair!") and the third (the lovers on the urn are far above "All breathing human passion . . . That leaves . . . A burning forehead, and a parching tongue"). In the fourth stanza, however, the speaker takes a fresh look at the urn, and his attitude changes by implication to a final decision in favor of earthly life. The procession of priest, heifer, and townspeople is stopped forever midway between an attractive destination (a "green altar") and an attractive source (the "little town by river or sea shore, / Or mountain-built with peaceful citadel"), and the permanent emptiness of the unseen town strikes the speaker as unbearably sad:

> And, little town, thy streets for evermore
>   Will silent be; and not a soul to tell
>   Why thou art desolate, can e'er return.   (38–40)

The perpetual midwayness of the procession (similar to a state described as "Purgatory blind" in the verse epistle to J. H. Reynolds, l. 80) reflects back on the situation of the piper, the lovers, and the trees, where process is frozen to a standstill and there is no fulfillment. "Desolate" in line 40 is the counterpart of "forlorn" in *Ode to a Nightingale*. It brings the speaker back to his sole self, and at the beginning of the final stanza he addresses the urn not as living entity but as artifact: it is now an "Attic shape," an "attitude," "overwrought" with "brede" of "marble" figures and trees, a "silent form," a "Cold Pastoral." Like the nightingale, it has offered a tentative ideal—momentarily "teas-[ing]" the speaker "out of thought"—but has also led the speaker to understand the shortcomings of the ideal. The final lines present a special problem in interpretation,[5] but it is clear that, while

[5] See Appendix III.

the urn is not entirely rejected at the end, its value lies in its character as a work of art, not in its being a possible substitute for life in the actual world. However punctuated, the urn's "message" amounts to what the speaker has come to realize in his speculations—that the only beauty accessible to mortal man exists "on earth." The urn is "a friend to man" for helping him to arrive at this conclusion through just such ponderings as we have witnessed in the course of the poem.

Ode on Melancholy, the most logically constructed of the odes, instead of following the flight-and-return pattern of the two preceding poems, enjoins against making the trip. "Go *not* to Lethe": the first stanza tells what not to do "when the melancholy fit shall fall," and beginning with forgetfulness and progressing through narcotics to poisons and death the images represent various anodynes to escape the unhappiness of the mortal condition. (Flying off to join the nightingale in the forest and entering into the life on the urn are the counterparts in the poems just discussed.) The anodynes are rejected because they shut out pleasure as well as pain: "For shade to shade will come too drowsily, / And drown the wakeful anguish of the soul." The second stanza advises what to do instead:

> Then glut thy sorrow on a morning rose,
> Or on the rainbow of the salt sand-wave,
> Or on the wealth of globed peonies;
> Or if thy mistress some rich anger shows,
> Emprison her soft hand, and let her rave,
> And feed deep, deep upon her peerless eyes

—that is, seize and experience the beauty of the transient natural and human world as fully as one can. The third stanza gives a rationale for these prescriptions (and, for that matter, a "doctrinal" basis for the other odes and poems of 1819 more generally). The pleasures and pains of life are inextricably bound up together: beauty and the melancholy awareness that beauty must die, joy and the simultaneous fading of joy, "aching Pleasure" and its instant turning to poison—all are inseparable, and one either accepts the pleasure-pain complexity or renounces life altogether. Of the alternatives given—the insensibility of narcosis and death in the first stanza and the bursting of "Joy's grape against his palate fine" toward the end of the third—the latter is obviously to be preferred.[6]

The last of the odes, and the least argumentative, though nonetheless deeply philosophical, *To Autumn* may be thought of as written out of the experience of the earlier poems. From beginning to end it celebrates the world of process—of "maturing," "ripeness," "budding"—not with innocent delight in the beauties of nature, but rather with a mature understanding that (to quote Wordsworth) this is "the very world, which is the world / Of all of us,—the place where, in the end, / We find our happiness, or not at all!" (*The Prelude,* XI.142-144). A momentary yearning for the otherworlds of the nightingale and the urn is expressed at the beginning of the third stanza: "Where are the songs of Spring? Ay, where are they?" But it is immediately put down by the next line, "Think not of them, thou hast thy music too," and the remainder of the poem, even while hinting of death among the noises of life, is unambiguously affirmative. The imagination is now devoted not to visionary flights but to a detailed examining of every natural sight and sound at hand, and the focus and attitude show the speaker reconciled to the real world he lives in.

II

In explaining how Keats, at the age of twenty-three, arrived at the maturity he shows in the poems just discussed, it is not en-

---

[6] This is true even though the burster of Joy's grape ends up "among [Melancholy's] cloudy trophies hung." In the last two lines, the emphasis should be on "taste"—rich experiencing—and I take "cloudy" here as an adjective of approval, meaning something like "exalted." The sense is that, while everyone has to succumb to Melancholy, the burster of Joy's grape is among the most worthy of her conquests.

tirely fanciful to view his over-all development in terms of just such a structure as we have seen in the best of the odes—a beginning flight from the real toward the ideal, a thoroughgoing imaginative assessment of the ideal, and a final return to the real. The poems of the 1817 volume—which are mainly about the question of whether Keats can and should be a poet, and which proceed from hesitancy to affirmation and the dedication to a ten-year program of development that, as it turns out, he had to condense into less than half that time—show many of the same thematic concerns that dominate the mature poems. There are above all the interest in perception and vision, the many contrasts of earthly and heavenly states, and the reiterated idea that imagination can serve as a bridge from one to the other. Keats first enters into vision in the twenty-ninth line of the opening poem (*I stood tiptoe*), and there are more ambitious excursions in the middle poem (the epistle *To My Brother George*) and the concluding piece (*Sleep and Poetry*). The attempts are sometimes tentative and awkward, but there is no doubt that in writing the poems Keats was (for poetic purposes at least) affirming literal belief in a commonplace of the day, the stock metaphor of visionary flight. Most of these poems were written in 1816, and in the pattern of Keats's career they may be taken collectively as fledgling ascent.

Endymion, which Keats began in April 1817, a month after his first volume was published, and completed in first draft at the end of November of the same year, represents his longest excursion in the realm of the ideal. It is the poem he had to write in order to begin freeing himself of the stock belief that informs the early poems. The allegorical narrative, which up to a point follows the classical myth of Endymion and the moon-goddess Cynthia, and may be read in part as a reply to Shelley's *Alastor,* which was published in the year before, is basically a simple one: a shepherd prince becomes enamored of an unknown goddess who visits him in a dream; turning his back on the world, he sets forth in quest of a reunion with her, and wanders through

caverns, under the ocean, and through the air; after several adventures, he meets and falls in love with an Indian maiden, and
vows to give up his pursuit of the goddess—whereupon the
maiden reveals that she is Cynthia in disguise, and the two are
blissfully reunited. Into this story Keats weaves a complexity of
themes: the idea of "fellowship with essence" (a kind of imaginative identification with things outside oneself that leads, at its
highest reach, to union with the ideal); the conflict of solitude
and self-love with humanitarian concerns; the opposing claims of
human and immortal existence; and several others.[7] In the first
and fourth books, however, the overriding preoccupation is the
question of the authenticity of dreams, which here as in most of
Keats's subsequent poems are meant to symbolize the visionary
imagination.

Toward the end of Book I, in an especially significant exchange
with his worldly-minded sister, Peona, who wants him to give up
his quest ("how light / Must dreams themselves be. . . . Why
pierce high-fronted honour to the quick / For nothing but a
dream?"—754–760), Endymion goes to great lengths to justify
the reality of the dream he is bent on pursuing (769 ff.). Keats
refers to this argument in the often-cited letter to Benjamin
Bailey (22 November 1817) when he affirms his belief in "the
authenticity of the Imagination"—"What the imagination seizes
as Beauty must be truth. . . . The Imagination may be compared
to Adam's dream [in *Paradise Lost,* Book VIII]—he awoke and
found it truth" (*Letters,* I, 184–185). Toward the end of his wanderings, however, Endymion has grave doubts:

> I have clung
> To nothing, lov'd a nothing, nothing seen
> Or felt but a great dream! . . .
>   . . . gone and past
> Are cloudy phantasms. Caverns lone, farewel!
> And air of visions, and the monstrous swell

[7] See "On the Interpretation of *Endymion,*" above.

Of visionary seas! No, never more
Shall airy voices cheat me. . . .   (IV.636–654)

As a matter of biographical fact, Keats wrote these lines very shortly after sending the letter to Bailey. It is of course Endymion who is speaking, at the height of his perplexity in finding himself in love with both a visionary goddess and one who he thinks is a mortal maiden, but the genuine fervency of the denial contrasts sharply with the affirmation of certainty in the letter. Forced to choose between the earthly and the ideal, Endymion renounces the ideal, and is saved only when the two turn out to be the same. It seems clear that he had to come to terms with human existence before he could be "Ensky'd" at the end; on the evidence of the poem, the way to heaven lies in earthly, not visionary, experiences.

The year 1818 marks an important turning point in Keats's mental life. Though hints, and occasionally more than hints, of skepticism were written into the first draft of *Endymion,* it was in the winter of 1817–18 that Keats himself noticed what he described as "a little change . . . in my intellect lately" (*Letters,* I, 214). Already tired of the poem before he finished it, he grew increasingly discontented as he revised it and copied it out for the printer (between January and the middle of March 1818), and several influences combined to turn him further against the kind of romance it represented: conversation and correspondence with the serious-minded Bailey; careful reading of Wordsworth; the attractiveness of the comic sense of Fielding and Smollett; and a new appreciation of the tragic sense of Shakespeare. The change shows itself in a number of short poems written during the winter, perhaps most notably in the sonnet *On Sitting Down to Read King Lear Once Again* (January), in which he dismisses "Romance" as a "barren dream." Toward the end of March, in the verse epistle to J. H. Reynolds, he struggles with the relationship of imagination to "the lore of good and ill" and describes a terrifying vision he has had of nature's cruelty, "an eternal fierce destruction"; the middle section speaks of the inadequacy of dreaming, the failure of the visionary imagination, and Keats's inability to find a healthy alternative. Between February and April he wrote *Isabella,* in which courtly-love romance and the "simple plaining of a minstrel's song" give over to what Keats considered a tough-minded modern account of the "wormy circumstance" of Lorenzo's death and Isabella's derangement.[8] In the summer of this year his brother George emigrated to America, and Keats set out on a walking tour of the English Lakes and Scotland that exposed him not only to the glories of nature but to the realities of rural poverty. The serious poems written during this tour continue to worry about the imagination (in the sonnet *On Visiting the Tomb of Burns,* "Fickly imagination & sick pride" cast a "dead hue" upon "The real of Beauty")[9] and to assert the impossibility of any permanent escape from the world (as in *Lines Written in the Highlands,* ll. 29–40). In the autumn Keats began work on the fragmentary epic *Hyperion,* which breaks off with the deification of Apollo—symbol of the humanitarian poet—through recognition and sympathetic understanding of the pain and misery of mortal life. At the beginning of December his brother Tom died.

The rapid growing-up that attended the intellectual and emotional experiences of 1818 goes far to account for what would otherwise be a paradox—that the more Keats saw of the sobering realities, the more favorable his attitude toward life in the world became as it is structured in his poems. The early work of 1816–17 (*Poems* and *Endymion*) proposed a visionary seeking after higher truth that we now view as romantic escapism. But as Keats confronted existence more openly, the simple escapism came to be rejected, and the poems of his maturity—by which one means those brilliant products, one after another, of a single year, 1819—

---

[8] See "Keats and Romance," the third essay in the present volume.

[9] I am quoting from the text established by J. C. Maxwell, "Keats's Sonnet on the Tomb of Burns," *Keats-Shelley Journal,* IV (1955), 77–80.

pose serious conflicts that are resolved, when they are resolved at
all, by acceptance of the pleasure-pain complexity of mortal life.
Beginning in January, with *The Eve of St. Agnes,* which depicts
the plight of a hoodwinked maiden who mistakenly thinks she
can separate the pleasures from the pain of life by following a
superstitious ritual and dreaming about them, Keats hit his stride.
The Eve of St. Agnes was followed by *The Eve of Saint Mark*
(February), in which another hoodwinked maiden similarly cuts
herself off from the realities of life by investing all her interests
and emotions in the legend of a long-dead martyr.[10] *La Belle
Dame sans Merci* (April) shows a wretched knight-at-arms unable to recover from a ghastly visionary experience. Then in April
and May come the odes—*Psyche, Nightingale, Grecian Urn,* and
probably also *Melancholy.* In the summer Keats wrote *Lamia,* in
which still another hoodwinked dreamer, like all the others unable to shed his human nature, suffers frustration and death
through his engrossment in a visionary ideal, as represented by
his love affair with the snake-woman Lamia. *The Fall of Hyperion,* which Keats began in the summer and gave up late in
September, two days after writing *To Autumn,* is also about the
dangers of dreaming (though in this work the concept is more
specifically connected with the writing of poetry). "The poet
and the dreamer are distinct," Moneta tells the poet, in a passage
that may serve as an epitome of the position Keats had arrived
at—"Diverse, sheer opposite, antipodes. / The one pours out a
balm upon the world, / The other vexes it" (I.199–202). To carry
out the analogy between the over-all career and the structure of
his odes, Keats began his descent from the ideal in the winter
of 1817–18, and by 1819 he was firmly grounded in the realities of
the actual world. The central point of the poems of 1819, from
The Eve of St. Agnes on, is that mortal man cannot escape his
mortality, and that dreaming and the mental process it stands

[10] See "The Hoodwinking of Madeline" and "The Meaning of 'Poor
Cheated Soul' in *The Eve of Saint Mark,*" earlier in the present volume.

for, a too exclusive commitment to the visionary imagination, produce only unhappiness. Keats's dreamers of this year either come to grief through their delusions or they learn their lesson and wake up. In the best of the odes the dreamers wake up.

A brief glance at the order of poems in Keats's final volume, published in July 1820, may serve as a basis for summary. The contents are as follows:

Lamia	*Ode* ["Bards of Passion and of Mirth"]
Isabella	*Lines on the Mermaid Tavern*
The Eve of St. Agnes	*Robin Hood*
Ode to a Nightingale	*To Autumn*
Ode on a Grecian Urn	*Ode on Melancholy*
Ode to Psyche	*Hyperion, a Fragment*
Fancy	

Arranged as they are, the poems show a progressive abandonment of the ideal and acceptance of the natural world, and a gradual movement from irresolution to resolution. *Lamia* sets forth the concern of nearly the entire volume—a clear (and in this poem unreconcilable) opposition between the ideal and the real, with dreaming as a metaphor for the mortal Lycius' involvement in an illusory ideal. *Isabella* and *The Eve of St. Agnes* anticipate the attitude of poems to follow by bringing a realistic view of things to bear on "old Romance." *Ode to a Nightingale* pictures an imaginative and unsuccessful attempt to merge with the supernatural (the "immortal" nightingale is no natural bird until the very end, and as such it has the same status as the fairy creatures and goddesses that bewitch other Keatsian dreamers from Endymion through the knight of *La Belle Dame* and Lycius —even Porphyro in *The Eve of St. Agnes* is associated with fairies and magic). *Ode on a Grecian Urn* shows the same attempt to escape into the realm of art, and *Ode to Psyche* (with its perhaps countering companion *Fancy*) projects an excursion into "some untrodden region" of the mind. The next three poems journey into the past as still another realm of escape, but the tone is light, and there is an awareness throughout that "those days are gone away" (*Robin Hood*). Then come the two final odes, *To Autumn* and *Melancholy,* with their focus on the natural world and unequivocal acceptance of it. Having rejected or found wanting the supernatural, art, the mind, and the past, the poet has only nature left; but the tone of these last poems makes clear that nature suffices. At the conclusion, as if to show what this maturing might have led to, *Hyperion* depicts the "dying into life" of the Apollo-poet through "Knowledge enormous" of the human condition. Apollo's reign, like Keats's career, is terminated just as it gets under way, and since Keats knew he was mortally ill when he assembled and arranged the poems for publication, it seems likely that he himself saw the parallel. The poem breaks off in mid-sentence, and we are left with a row and a half of asterisks, and then the two words, "The End."

III

Keats was not widely read in his own day. Chopped up by the *Blackwood's* and *Quarterly* reviewers (mainly because of his association with the political radical Leigh Hunt), he aimed for posterity and a circle of friends who, after his death, worked heroically to make his poetry better known. The publication of Richard Monckton Milnes's *Life, Letters, and Literary Remains, of John Keats* (1848), based on unpublished poems, letters, and reminiscences supplied by those friends, finally brought Keats a measure of the fame he deserved, and as his life and poems were read and reread in the latter half of the century he came to be nearly idolized by the Victorians. Generally he was admired for the wrong reasons, as a poet of art for art's sake, the sensualist poet, the painter of rich pictures and the burster of Joy's grape, sometimes even with cayenne pepper on his tongue. It is a view that one sees in serious criticism as late as a generation ago—for example, in H. W. Garrod's statement that "I think him the great poet he is only when the senses capture him, when he finds truth in beauty, that is to say, when he does not trouble to find truth at all" [11]—and in popular journalism even today. The Humanist critics of the 1920's included him in their attack on Romantic escapism, reading *Ode to a Nightingale* as if it ended in the middle of the fourth stanza and *Ode on a Grecian Urn* as if it ended with the third stanza. Then around 1925, when Amy Lowell's massive biography was published, to be followed in the next year by Clarence D. Thorpe's *The Mind of John Keats,* critics began giving serious attention to Keats the thinker: the letters on imagination (22 November 1817), Negative Capability (21, 27[?] December 1817, 27 October 1818), life as a "Mansion of Many Apartments" (3 May 1818), and the world as a "vale of Soul-making" (21 April 1819) suddenly became important. Close reading by the New Critics in the 1930's and '40's further enhanced his stature, and fresh interpretations of the odes and other poems poured forth to lift him almost to metaphysical heights.

Keats's reputation, which continues to grow, has never been better. With the help of Douglas Bush, W. J. Bate, and others, we have learned to take a middle view between the sensualist and the idealist, seeing Keats primarily as humanist—the honest confronter of difficult human problems, and the one of all the Romantics who least took refuge in some outdated system in order to solve them. Keats read human nature accurately, and his best poems picture the truth of the mind's impassioned questing. "Some desire is necessary to keep life in motion," pronounces Imlac, in one of those eternal verities of Johnson's *Rasselas* (ch. VIII). The nine words may be taken to explain why the situation on the Grecian urn is rejected, once the impossibility of fulfillment has been grasped. Wordsworth says the same thing in his apostrophe to Imagination in Book VI of *The Prelude:*

[11] *Keats,* 2nd ed. (Oxford, 1939), p. 61.

> With hope it is, hope that can never die,
> Effort, and expectation, and desire,
> And something evermore about to be.   (606–608)

Endymion's speech about the warrior who, as soon as he captures one "fancied city of delight," must immediately set about taking another, and then another, again makes the point:

> But this is human life: the war, the deeds,
> The disappointment, the anxiety,
> Imagination's struggles, far and nigh,
> All human; bearing in themselves this good,
> That they are still the air, the subtle food,
> To make us feel existence, and to show
> How quiet death is.   (*Endymion,* II.153–159)

And as Keats put it in prose, in a letter to Bailey of 13 March 1818, just as he was finishing the revision of *Endymion* and was well launched on that year of accelerated growing-up, "every mental pursuit takes its reality and worth from the ardour of the pursuer—being in itself a nothing" (*Letters,* I, 242). It is above all this ardent "mental pursuit" that we see in Keats's poems, and his steady understanding where the reality lies that we especially admire. In the end, the "sudden rightnesses" of the odes put the mind just where it should be, in that delicate balance (as Wallace Stevens describes it in *Of Modern Poetry*) "below which it cannot descend, / Beyond which it has no will to rise."

Keats, Wordsworth, and "Romanticism"

I

I still have, in some old notes from a sophomore survey of English literature taken two decades ago, a table of comparisons that the instructor put up on the blackboard one day, more than halfway through the course, at the point where we had just finished the eighteenth century and were plunging ahead into the nineteenth. If I copied correctly, it looked like this:

NEOCLASSICISM—18th century	ROMANTICISM—19th century to the present
Reason and sense of fact	Sentiment, passion, mystery
Intellect and common sense . . .	Imagination and intuition
Restraint in feeling	Emotional license
Conformity to custom	Individualism
Obedience to strict literary rules of classic authors	Free choice of literary forms
Neoclassicism	Revival of medievalism
Faith in established church . . .	Protestantism and dissent
Conservative politics	Revolution
Favoritism to privileged classes .	Social reform, rise of lower classes, Democracy

I dutifully memorized the table (as was the custom then), and did the reading in the course. On the final examination, to answer some question about the shift in values between the eighteenth and nineteenth centuries, I rehashed the generalizations from the table I had "learned," and received an A for my secretarial skills.

One of the poems we "read" in the course—though I realize
now that probably none of the students grasped much of what
was going on in it—was Wordsworth's shortest Lucy lyric:

> A slumber did my spirit seal;
>   I had no human fears:
> She seemed a thing that could not feel
>   The touch of earthly years.
>
> No motion has she now, no force;
>   She neither hears nor sees;
> Rolled round in earth's diurnal course,
>   With rocks, and stones, and trees.

Possibly a few of us understood that Wordsworth was describing
a universal situation—shock and grief over the unexpected loss of a
loved one. But the New Criticism of the preceding decade and
a half had not yet influenced the sophomore survey at my university, and the things we neglected to consider would make a
long list: for example, the poem's subject (mortality, mutability
in human life), the main focus (the delusion of the speaker, and
the sudden shedding of delusion), the principal metaphor (slumber followed by awakening), the structure (a two-part, then/now
affair), the language of physics and astronomy in the second
stanza, the poem's economy, and so on. What we most especially
did not discuss was the relationship of the poem to the table of
comparisons on the blackboard. There are "sentiment, passion,
mystery" *and* "reason and sense of fact" in the poem, "imagination and intuition" *and* "intellect and common sense"—or rather,
to locate these things slightly more precisely, there are the supposed Romantic "sentiment, passion, mystery" and "imagination
and intuition" in the first quatrain, and the supposed Neoclassic
"reason and sense of fact" and "intellect and common sense" in
the second. Far from illustrating "emotional license," the poem is
superbly restrained in feeling. As for the fifth item in the table
of comparisons, the traditional 4-3-4-3 quatrains hardly exemplify

"free choice of literary forms." There is nothing in the poem about conformity versus individualism, or about classicism, medievalism, religion,[1] or politics.

According, then, to the first, second, third, and fifth items in the table (the others have no bearing), *A slumber did my spirit seal* is more Neoclassic than Romantic, or may be said to show Romanticism put down by Neoclassicism. But the poem was written by one whom we are accustomed to think of as a major "Romantic" poet, and it does not stand out in his work as untypical of the whole. It is a common situation in literary history, a product of the gap between the close readers of literary works, who distrust categorizing, and the historical categorizers, who do not read closely: the generalizations do not describe the particular poem, the poem does not fit the descriptions, and something is amiss. The items under "Romanticism" in the table might appropriately apply to a combination of, say, *Christabel, Lara,* and *Epipsychidion.* They do not, taken together, describe the leading characteristics of the best poems written by Wordsworth and Keats.

In this kind of confrontation, which I use merely as a convenient example, the historian has a choice of (once again) redefining Romanticism, or declaring that Wordsworth was not a Romantic. The former is the better alternative, since, unlike the generalizations, the poem does and Wordsworth did really exist as part and product of a historical period, and it is easier to change a hypothesis than a fact. And there is still some point in trying to say more accurately what English Romanticism *was,* if only as a help toward the better understanding of a number

---

[1] I am aware that some critics find a hint of pantheism in the last two lines: the loved one by her death becomes a part of nature. But I think this suggestion is nullified by the striking effect of the final images, all of which emphasize the fact that she is thoroughly *dead*—as insensible and motionless as rocks and stones and trees.

of important works of the period.[2] Very briefly, my beginning position in this essay is the following. While the common term "romanticism" embraces many things, in one large sense it stands for a body of ideas and attitudes that we do not—or no longer (or perhaps never did)—hold true or valuable.[3] To an unfortunate degree the pejorative connotations of the term have become attached to general descriptions of the English poets of the first part of the nineteenth century. As a result, the poets are sometimes thought to have believed that flowers enjoy the air they breathe, or that a man can escape the conditions of mortality by joining the figures on an urn or a nightingale in the forest; and for such reasons their poems are read—or theoretically ought to be read—almost as historical curiosities. I feel that many of the usual generalizations about English Romanticism are based on second-rate poets and poems,[4] and that the generalizations foster

[2] Several hundred books and articles have attempted to define "Romanticism." Robert F. Gleckner's and Gerald E. Enscoe's *Romanticism: Points of View,* 2nd ed. (Englewood Cliffs, N.J., 1970), is a well-chosen selection of writings on the subject. The most useful works for the present essay have been Lascelles Abercrombie, *Romanticism* (London, 1926); Albert Gérard, "On the Logic of Romanticism," *Essays in Criticism,* VII (1957), 262–273 (see also Gérard's *English Romantic Poetry,* Berkeley and Los Angeles, 1968); Morse Peckham, "Toward a Theory of Romanticism: II. Reconsiderations," *Studies in Romanticism,* I (1961), 1–8; and Earl R. Wasserman, "The English Romantics: The Grounds of Knowledge," *Studies in Romanticism,* IV (1964), 17–34.

[3] Those that we do still value—such as the importance of the individual, the identity of self, political liberalism or radicalism, various concepts in art (e.g., concreteness, particularity, symbolism)—we do not consider "romantic," even though they may have emerged or been strengthened in the Romantic period. In this sense, "romantic" means to us just what it meant to Dr. Johnson or Jane Austen: unrealistic, unreasonable, impractical, and the like.

[4] To cite a recent example, Northrop Frye's *A Study of English Romanticism* (New York, 1968) draws its conclusions from an examination of Beddoes' *Death's Jest-Book,* Shelley's *Prometheus Unbound,* and Keats's *Endymion.*

misreadings of the first-rate. In the best work of the two most
important poets of the period, Wordsworth and Keats, there is a
large measure of realism that by the prevailing standards should
be called *"anti-romantic."* In the following sections I hope to
avoid both the problem of circularity in definition and the confusion inherent in the idea of calling a Romantic poet "anti-
romantic."

II

I begin with some generalizations which, if they are just as sweep-
ing and naïve as the ones in the blackboard table, are nevertheless
valid for my purposes since the writers I am concerned with actually believed them. In the Renaissance and earlier it was taken
for granted that man and nature combined in a perfect unity held
together by God. With the Enlightenment of the seventeenth and
eighteenth centuries there occurred a systematic breakdown of this
simple unity. The new theology—Deism—removed God from an
active role in everyday affairs, seeing him of primary importance
only at the time of the original Creation, where he is thought to
have done a good job (one writer, congratulating God on having
placed man's elbow at just the right distance between hand and
shoulder, says, "Let us adore, then, glass in hand, God's benevo-
lent wisdom. Let us adore and drink!"). The "new philosophy"
or new science—Newton's description of the physical universe—
divested nature of both life and purpose, rendering it mere dead
matter, the "inanimate cold world" of Coleridge's *Dejection: An
Ode* and the "universe of death" of *The Prelude* (XIV.160). The
new psychology—the associationalism of Locke and Hartley—
viewed the human mind as a mechanism. Thus, where before
God and nature and man were meaningfully interrelated, now
God was out of the picture and the mind had only the most
mechanical connection with a lifeless external world.

The major concern of the Romantics was to deny or else find
remedies or compensations for this breakdown of unity—to dis-

cover some new theory or explanation to justify their ordinary human *feelings* that unity did exist, that (in some writers at least) God was not "dead" in the deistical sense, that nature was more than inanimate matter, and that the mind was more than a mechanism. Now rather than find meaning in nature (as was possible in the old unity), it became necessary for man to create it. But the psychological theorists denied the mind's ability to create: sense impressions could be linked and combined, simple sensations built into complex, but nothing new could result. Consider the following:

as we have no Imagination, whereof we have not formerly had Sense, in whole, or in parts; so we have no Transition from one Imagination to another, whereof we never had the like before in our Senses. (Hobbes, *Leviathan,* 1651, Part I, ch. III)

it is not in the Power of the most exalted Wit, or enlarged Understanding, by any quickness or variety of Thought, to *invent or frame one new simple* Idea in the Mind. . . . [Man's] Power, however managed by Art and Skill, reaches no farther, than to compound and divide the Materials that are made to his Hand; but can do nothing towards the making the least Particle of new Matter. . . . (Locke, *An Essay Concerning Humane Understanding,* 1690, Book II, ch. II)

We cannot indeed have a single Image in the Fancy that did not make its first Entrance through the Sight. . . . (Addison, *Spectator* No. 411, 1712)

every succeeding Thought is the Result either of some new Impression, or of an Association with the preceding. (Hartley, *Observations on Man,* 1749, Part I, ch. III, sect. v)

this power of the imagination is incapable of producing any thing absolutely new; it can only vary the disposition of those ideas which it has received from the senses. (Burke, *A Philosophical Enquiry into the Origin of Our Ideas of the Sublime and Beautiful,* 2nd ed., 1759, Introduction)

In the wildest flights of *fancy,* it is probable that no single idea occurs to us but such as had a connection with some other impression or idea, previously existing in the mind; and what we call *new thoughts* are only new combinations, of old simple ideas, or decompositions of complex ones. (Priestley, *Hartley's Theory of the Human Mind,* 1775, Introductory Essay II)

The extracts all say the same thing, that the human mind is incapable of creating anything new. They describe a situation in which, says Coleridge in *Biographia Literaria,* chapter VI, arguing against Hartley, "our whole life would be divided between the despotism of outward impressions, and that of senseless and passive memory." The fact would be oppressive to poets of any age, but was especially so to the Romantics, whose experiences with and urges toward creativity did not square with the theory. To reintegrate the elements of the old unity—and, for that matter, to do anything new in poetry—creativity had to be justified.

It is in dealing with this problem concerning the mind's creativity, and in positing imagination as a means of remedy, that the major Romantics—regardless of the specific tendencies of their answers—genuinely have something in common besides their temporal coexistence. Each of the writers tried in his own way to circumvent the negative decree represented by the extracts from Hobbes through Priestley given above, and their attempts may be seen to take one of two forms, according to whether their theories of imagination accepted or denied Locke's and Hartley's [5] descriptions of the way the mind works. One of these forms is the *naturalized imagination* (so named because it works with visible things in the natural world), which operates within Locke's and Hartley's terms but nevertheless, on the basis of simple common-sense observation, is found to be authentically creative. It is

[5] From here on, I refer specifically to Locke and Hartley to represent the psychological theorists' negative view concerning the mind's creativity—Locke because of his steady preeminence throughout the eighteenth century, and Hartley because of his increasing influence toward the end of the century (Priestley's 1775 abridgment of *Observations on Man* appeared in a second edition in 1790, and the complete *Observations* was reissued twice in 1791 and again in 1801 and 1810).

best exemplified in the Wordsworthian (and Coleridgean) concept of "creative sensibility," discussed in the next section. The other is the *visionary imagination,* which violates Locke's and Hartley's terms by going beyond the senses in search of invisible things. Very crudely, this involves a Platonic or idealist or rationalist notion of penetrating to a higher realm, to something "above" or other than the everyday world of experience. One sees this especially in Blake and Shelley, and also in Keats, whom for my special purposes I shall use to exemplify it in section IV.

III

Wordsworth's type of naturalized imagination, involving the mind's ability to create as it perceives, to manipulate and modify sensations, may be seen quite plainly in the boat-stealing episode of *The Prelude* (I.357–400).[6] Already feeling guilty, the boy takes a boat that does not belong to him and rows out into the lake, his eye fixed, as he sits facing the stern of the boat, "Upon the summit of a craggy ridge, / The horizon's utmost boundary." As he rows farther from the shore, his angle of vision changes, and he discovers a mountain peak *rising* behind the ridge—

> a huge peak, black and huge,
> As if with voluntary power instinct
> Upreared its head. I struck and struck again,
> And growing still in stature the grim shape
> Towered up between me and the stars, and still,
> For so it seemed, with purpose of its own

[6] The following discussion incorporates some paragraphs of my introduction to *William Wordsworth: Selected Poems and Prefaces* (Boston, 1965). For more recent discussions of Wordsworth's concept of imagination see Robert Langbaum, "The Evolution of Soul in Wordsworth's Poetry," *PMLA,* LXXXII (1967), 265–272 (reprinted in Langbaum's *The Modern Spirit: Essays on the Continuity of Nineteenth- and Twentieth-Century Literature,* New York, 1970, pp. 18–36); and James A. W. Heffernan, *Wordsworth's Theory of Poetry: The Transforming Imagination* (Ithaca and London, 1969).

And measured motion like a living thing,
  Strode after me.   (378–385)

We know, of course, and so did Wordsworth when he wrote down the incident (note the qualifiers "As if," "so it seemed," "*like* a living thing"), that the peak was always there, mindless and unmoving. But the boy's imagination endows it with life, motion, a "purpose of its own." For him it is a moral agent; "With trembling oars" he returns the boat to its mooring-place, and for days and nights afterward the fearful experience affects him. Clearly he has mentally added a great deal to the scene that surrounds him; and there is no idea of an inherently active universe, no hint of a religious or philosophical basis for what happens—it is, rather, a perfectly natural experience in the process of growing up.

In *The Prelude* Wordsworth's first theoretical statement about the faculty of imagination that he praises so highly comes in the passage beginning "Blest the infant Babe" in Book II (232 ff.). Almost from the first, in the simplest acts of perception—recognizing the "one dear Presence," his mother, out of the separate parts of an arm, a breast, an eye, and so on, or constructing the idea that a flower, because it is associated with his mother's affection, is beautiful—the infant mind unifies as it perceives, organizing and adding to the sensations taken in:

> For feeling has to him imparted power
> That through the growing faculties of sense
> Doth like an agent of the one great Mind
> Create, creator and receiver both,
> Working but in alliance with the works
> Which it beholds.—Such, verily, is the first
> Poetic spirit of our human life,
> By uniform control of after years,
> In most, abated or suppressed; in some,
> Through every change of growth and of decay,
> Pre-eminent till death.   (255–265)

Practically all the most characteristic Wordsworthian ideas are
here: that this unifying, modifying, new-creating "power" is
based on (but not restricted to) the "growing faculties of sense";
that it is a god-like power (cf. "Creation and divinity itself" in
the summary passage at III.174); that it works in alliance with
nature in a giving-receiving process (the "ennobling interchange"
talked about at the end of Book XIII); that it operates at its best
in youth, and fades (except in those few who remain strong, who
therefore become "poets," regardless of whether or not they write
poetry) in the course of growing up. The power is called here
"the first / Poetic spirit," a few lines later "this infant sensibility"
(270), and still later "My first creative sensibility" (360). The last
term is the most appropriate, since it embraces both sensation and
creation, denoting a process whereby outer and inner are combined.

   As he most frequently writes about it in his poems, Wordsworth's concept of imagination is identical with the "shaping
spirit" of Coleridge's *Dejection: An Ode* (1802)—

> O Lady! we receive but what we give,
> And in our life alone does Nature live:
> Ours is her wedding garment, ours her shroud!
>   And would we aught behold, of higher worth,
> Than that inanimate cold world allowed
> To the poor loveless ever-anxious crowd,
>   Ah! from the soul itself must issue forth
> A light, a glory, a fair luminous cloud
>   Enveloping the Earth—   (47–55)

and it is very much like the combined faculties of primary and
secondary imagination as they are defined in Coleridge's brief remarks at the end of chapter XIII of *Biographia Literaria*:

The IMAGINATION . . . I consider either as primary, or secondary. The
primary IMAGINATION I hold to be the living Power and prime Agent
of all human Perception, and as a repetition in the finite mind of the

eternal act of creation in the infinite I ᴀᴍ. The secondary Imagination I consider as an echo of the former, co-existing with the conscious will, yet still as identical with the primary in the *kind* of its agency, and differing only in *degree,* and in the *mode* of its operation. It dissolves, diffuses, dissipates, in order to re-create; or where this process is rendered impossible, yet still at all events it struggles to idealize and to unify. It is essentially *vital,* even as all objects (*as* objects) are essentially fixed and dead.

Both Wordsworth and Coleridge employ images of projection (especially of light) and spreading abroad to describe this power: for example, "An auxiliar light / Came from my mind, which on the setting sun / Bestowed new splendour" (*The Prelude,* II.368–370); "moments awful . . . When power streamed from thee, and thy soul received / The light reflected, as a light bestowed" (Coleridge's *To William Wordsworth,* ll. 16–19, written after Wordsworth read *The Prelude* to him). The mind projects life, meaning, and value onto the external world in this giving-receiving process; without man, Wordsworth wrote in an early manuscript of *The Prelude,* "the Earth / Is valueless." [7] Hopkins has the same idea in *Hurrahing in Harvest:*

> These things, these things were here and but the beholder
>   Wanting; which two when they once meet,
> The heart rears wings bold and bolder
>   And hurls for him, O half hurls earth for him off under his feet.

And like Hopkins here, Wordsworth constantly uses the language of explosion and fireworks ("flash," "gleam," "burst") in recounting the most ordinary interactions of mind and nature.

Later in Book II of *The Prelude* Wordsworth entertains the idea that this unifying, new-creating faculty is responsible for a feeling of "one life" in the universe, a "sentiment of Being spread / O'er all," and that he coerces "all things into sympathy,"

[7] See *The Prelude,* ed. Ernest de Selincourt, 2nd ed., revised by Helen Darbishire (Oxford, 1959), p. 578.

transferring "To unorganic natures . . . My own enjoyments" (387-402). Here he offers an alternative possibility—that he "did converse / With things that really are"—but in Book III he is more decisive: he "spread [his] thoughts / And spread them with a wider creeping," and in return "felt / Incumbencies more awful, visitings / Of the Upholder of the tranquil soul"; "To every natural form, rock, fruit or flower, / Even the loose stones that cover the high-way, / I gave a moral life. . . . I had a world about me—'twas my own; / I made it" (116-145). It ought to be clear, even in these early books, that creative sensibility is not primarily a producer of mystic experiences. Wordsworth's immediate concern is always psychological; in the most impressive passages of the later books of *The Prelude,* the "spots of time" in Book XII and the ascent of Mt. Snowdon in Book XIV, no direct religious experience is involved.

The passage on "spots of time" (XII.208 ff.) is of crucial importance in showing Wordsworth's ultimate view of the greatness of man's mental powers. Its very simplicity may mislead us. Having told in the first eight books how his upbringing in nature led to a love of man, and in the next three (IX–XI) how this love fostered an interest in man's betterment through revolutionary activities in France, how his enthusiasm turned out to be invested in a defective cause, and how, as a result, his imagination was "impaired" until a return to nature (his sister leading him by the hand) effected a restoration, he now says that he "again / In Nature's presence stood . . . A sensitive being, a *creative* soul." He then goes on, beginning a new paragraph:

> There are in our existence spots of time,
> That with distinct pre-eminence retain
> A renovating virtue, whence . . .
>   . . . our minds
> Are nourished and invisibly repaired;
> A virtue, by which pleasure is enhanced,
> That penetrates, enables us to mount,

When high, more high, and lifts us up when fallen.
This efficacious spirit chiefly lurks
Among those passages of life that give
Profoundest knowledge to what point, and how,
The mind is lord and master—outward sense
The obedient servant of her will.   (208–223)

Two exemplifying incidents follow. In the first, Wordsworth tells
that once as a boy he became separated from his father's servant,
came to a place where a murderer had been hanged, and fled
from that to the bare common, where he saw "A naked pool
that lay beneath the hills, / The beacon on the summit, and,
more near, / A girl, who bore a pitcher on her head, / And
seemed with difficult steps to force her way / Against the blow-
ing wind"—an ordinary sight, Wordsworth says, and yet one of
"visionary dreariness" (249–256). Years later, when he returned
to the same spot with his loved one, the scene was transformed:

Upon the naked pool and dreary crags,
And on the melancholy beacon, fell
A spirit of pleasure and youth's golden gleam;
And think ye not with radiance more sublime
For these remembrances, and for the power
They had left behind?   (264–269)

The point is not just that his early fear made the landscape seem
dreary and his later happiness in love made it seem pleasant, but
that the later pleasure was heightened, "with radiance more sublime," *because* of its association with the earlier terror. The second
example again involves a mental combining—of the anticipation
of joy in going home for the Christmas holidays with the grief
and "chastisement" of his father's death ten days later—and the
emotions are again associated with elements of the landscape, a
single sheep and a blasted hawthorn. In representing the combination of sensations ("So feeling comes in aid / Of feeling,"
269–270) into something not inherent in the scene itself, both

passages illustrate how "The mind is lord and master" over outward sense. And in them, and similar recollected experiences,
Wordsworth thought he found an answer to a major problem
of the poem, "A more judicious knowledge of the worth / And
dignity of individual man" (XIII.80–81).

The most difficult task in understanding Wordsworth is that
of reconciling creative sensibility, as just described, with the in-
finity-questing imagination that takes on considerable prominence
in several passages of *The Prelude*. Wordsworth thought of them
as operations of the same faculty, and we do wrong to separate
them (especially by calling one fancy, the other imagination, on
the basis of distinctions that he made some years after writing his
major poems). But we are faced, no matter which way we turn,
with apparent contradictions: the state of being "laid asleep /
In body," for example, is at odds with "the language of the
sense" in *Tintern Abbey* (45–46, 108).

The solution to the difficulty turns, I think, on Wordsworth's
special meaning of "infinity," [8] which in Book VI of *The Prelude* he describes as "hope . . . expectation, and desire, / And
something evermore about to be" (606–608), and in Book XIV
symbolizes by "waters, torrents, streams / Innumerable, roaring
with one voice . . . voices issuing forth to silent light / In one

[8] In addition to Wordsworth's own works, some justification for this
paragraph lies in Locke's discussion "Of Infinity" (*An Essay Concerning
Humane Understanding,* Bk. II, ch. XVII)—e.g., "Space, Duration, and
Number, being capable of increase by repetition, leave in the Mind an *Idea*
of an endless room for more; nor can we conceive any where a stop to a
farther Addition or Progression, and so those *Ideas* alone lead our Minds
towards the Thought of Infinity"—and in David Hume's *Philosophical
Essays Concerning Human Understanding* (1748), Essay V: "There is
nothing more free than the Imagination of Man; and tho' it cannot exceed
that original Stock of Ideas, which is furnish'd by our internal and external
Senses, it has *unlimited* Power of mixing, compounding, separating and
dividing these Ideas" (italics mine). Shelley is thinking of the same thing
when, in a Lockean scheme, he refers to the *Alastor*-Poet's "desires to point
towards objects thus infinite [in "variety" of "modifications"] and unmea-
sured" (Preface to *Alastor*).

continuous stream" (59–74). In these passages infinity is the opposite of limitation or confinement; as an expression of freedom
it is specifically set against the tyranny of the senses, that "Single
vision & Newton's sleep" (Blake's terms) whereby the mind is
arrested and held captive by whatever the senses are immediately
taking in. In Wordsworth's thinking, creative sensibility is a
power of infinite possibilities (among which the feeling of God
or divine life in nature may be included). In Book II, for example,
the "growing faculties" of sense lead to "possible sublimity"—

> With growing faculties she [the "soul" or mind] doth aspire,
> With faculties still growing, feeling still
> That whatsoever point they gain, they yet
> Have something to pursue.   (319–322)

In Books VI and VII we are shown ways in which the natural
world leads the mind to an idea of something beyond nature:
"The immeasurable height / Of woods decaying, never to be de-
cayed, / The stationary blasts of waterfalls," and other images of
permanence are seen as "types and symbols of Eternity" (VI.624–
639); and "the everlasting streams and woods, / Stretched and
still stretching," and other impressions shape "The views and
aspirations of the soul / To majesty" (VII.745–756). In Book XIV
the "mind / That feeds upon infinity" is "sustained / By recog-
nitions of transcendent power, / In sense conducting to ideal
form" (70–76).

"Infinity," however, is not so important as the interplay of mind
and nature producing less supernatural effects. In the over-all
view, both nature and mind, both sensations and imagination
working upon those sensations, are necessary to the ideal human
condition. On the one hand, separated from "forms and images"
of nature, the mind loses itself in a "blank abyss" (VI.470), "in
endless dreams / Of sickliness, disjoining, joining, things / Without the light of knowledge" (VIII.435–437); on the other, overwhelmed by sensible impressions, by "the bodily eye . . . held

. . . In absolute dominion," the inner faculties are laid asleep
(XII.128–147)—either condition is bad. The ideal is

> A balance, an ennobling interchange
> Of action from without and from within;
> The excellence, pure function, and best power
> Both of the object seen, and eye that sees.   (XIII.375–378)

It is not necessary for nature to be alive or active in any magical
sense; it is enough that nature exists as a basis (in both perception and memory) on which the "excited spirit" can work its
infinite creations. The mind is lord and master, outward sense
the obedient servant; but both mind *and* outward sense ("action
from without") are essential in Wordsworth's "high argument"
in *The Recluse:*

> How exquisitely the individual Mind
> (And the progressive powers perhaps no less
> Of the whole species) to the external World
> Is fitted:—and how exquisitely, too—
> Theme this but little heard of among men—
> The external World is fitted to the Mind;
> And the creation (by no lower name
> Can it be called) which they with blended might
> Accomplish. . . .   (816–824)

This exquisite "fitting," enabling man to create as he perceives,
combining past impressions with new ones in the process of "interchange / Of action from without and from within," is Wordsworth's answer to the problem outlined in the preceding section.
In his view, creative sensibility *did* work to produce "something
new," and did so without violating Locke's and Hartley's terms.

IV

The other basic kind of imagination in the Romantic period deals
with invisible rather than visible things, and involves a supposedly
ennobling interchange of the mind not with "action from with-

out" but with action *from above*. This is sometimes called the "apocalyptic imagination" (especially by those studying Blake and Shelley). I have used the term "visionary imagination" in several earlier essays in this volume, and shall continue with it here. Keats's invisible bird in *Ode to a Nightingale* may serve as the epitomizing example: it and its dim forest habitat represent another world that is opposed to, and for part of the poem is superior to, the speaker's actual world of "weariness . . . fever . . . fret," sickness, aging, death, and the fading of love. The most basic opposition concerns the mortality of the speaker and the immortality of the bird, and, to put a complex matter very simply, the speaker wants to leave his own world and become part of the nightingale's. This he would do, and temporarily succeeds in doing, "on the viewless wings of Poesy." The imagination, in the first half of the poem at least, is thought of as a means of getting from the actual world to a higher and better (because more permanent) reality.

Keats's interest in the visionary imagination may be seen in many passages of his first volume, in which poetic activity itself is pictured as visionary flight. To illustrate to just what extent this process was a conventional notion of the day, I shall quote a lengthy passage from Leigh Hunt's *Politics and Poetics,* first published in 1811 and reprinted, in a volume that Keats surely knew, in 1815. Hunt's poem is subtitled "The Desperate Situation of a Journalist Unhappily Smitten with the Love of Rhyme," and represents in the following lines an interruptive poetic flight while Hunt is in the midst of political writing:

> But see! e'en now the Muse's charm prevails;
> The shapes [9] are moved, the stricken circle fails;

[9] These "shapes" are various fancied figures representing Hunt's "daily cares"—a "Blue Daemon," Nightmare, Headache, a goblin backbiter, and, worst of all, the printer's devil who comes for copy. The lines are quoted from *The Poetical Works of Leigh Hunt,* ed. H. S. Milford (London, 1923), pp. 142–143. Claude Lee Finney, *The Evolution of Keats's Poetry*

With backward grins of malice they retire,
Scared by her seraph looks and smiles of fire.
That instant, as the hindmost shuts the door,
The bursting sunshine smites the windowed floor;
Bursts too on every side the sparkling sound
Of birds abroad; th' elastic spirits bound;
And the fresh mirth of morning breathes around:
Away, ye clouds; dull politics, give place;
Off, cares, and wants, and threats, and all the race
Of foes to freedom and to laurelled leisure!—
To-day is for the Muse, and dancing Pleasure.

Oh for a seat in some poetic nook,
Just hid with trees, and sparkling with a brook,
Where through the quivering boughs the sunbeams shoot
Their arrowy diamonds upon flower and fruit,
While stealing airs come fuming o'er the stream,
And lull the fancy to a waking dream!
There shouldst thou come, O first of my desires,
What time the noon had spent its fiercer fires,
And all the bow'r, with checquered shadows strewn,
Glowed with a mellow twilight of its own.
There shouldst thou come, and there sometimes with thee
Might deign repair the staid Philosophy,
To taste thy fresh'ning brook, and trim thy groves,
And tell us what good task true glory loves.

I see it now!—I pierce the fairy glade,
And feel th' enclosing influence of the shade.
A thousand forms, that sport on summer eves,
Glance through the light, and whisper in the leaves,
While every bough seems nodding with a sprite,
And every air seems hushing the delight,
And the calm bliss, fixed on itself awhile,
Dimples the unconscious lips into a smile.

(Cambridge, Mass., 1936), I, 82–83, cites ll. 72–100 of this passage as a
source for Keats's epistle *To George Felton Mathew*.

Anon strange music breathes;—the fairies show
Their pranksome crowd; and in grave order go
Beside the water, singing, small and clear,
New harmonies unknown to mortal ear,
Caught upon moonlight nights from some nigh-wandering sphere.
I turn to them, and listen with fixed eyes,
And feel my spirits mount on winged ecstacies.   (59–100)

There are several things worth pausing over here—the imaginary visit to "some poetic nook" that does not really exist, the lulling of the fancy into "a waking dream," the ideas of *seeing* and *piercing,* the finding of a "fairy glade" where there is "strange music . . . New harmonies unknown to mortal ear," and especially, what makes the whole experience possible, the *mounting* of spirits "on winged ecstacies." Hunt is doing nothing new here; the various elements singled out were all part of a cliché or stock metaphor long established by the time he was writing (cf. "wildest flights of *fancy*" in the quotation from Priestley in section II, above). The significant point is that Keats, unlike Hunt, took the notion seriously and literally, as the poems published in 1817 show repeatedly.

Consider, for example, the opening poem of the 1817 volume. The mention of "greediest eye . . . pictur[ing] out . . . Guess-[ing]" in lines 15, 19, 22 of *I stood tip-toe* signals an activity that is prominent in Keats's poems from the beginning to the end of his short career. It is not entirely wrong to suggest that *the* Keatsian poetic process involves *seeing* up to a point and then *guessing* beyond that point (an obvious example would again be *Ode to a Nightingale,* in the middle stanzas especially, where the speaker sees certain things and then "cannot see . . . But . . . guess[es] . . ."). "Vision" is mentioned in line 26, and a long passage of the poem beginning with line 29 consists of an imagined (for Keats a "visionary") scene. The poetic process is linked with "lovely dreams" (120), also with being "uplifted from the world" (139), and later in the poem the teller of the story of Endymion and Cynthia is described as "bringing / Shapes from the invisible world, unearthly singing" (185–186), and "burst[ing] our mortal bars" to "search" "Into some won-d'rous region" (190–192). In writing down these visions, Keats's own "wand'ring spirit" has "soar[ed]" (242). All these terms— "vision," "dreams," "invisible world," "unearthly"—would quite properly go unnoticed in a Hunt poem; in Keats the words are of considerable importance.

I shall pass over various references to visionary experience in the shorter poems [10] in order to focus briefly on the second of the three epistles, *To My Brother George,* and the final poem of the volume, *Sleep and Poetry.* The epistle to George opens with a contrast between the "bewilder'd" brain, which sees "sheeted lightning" as just what it is in nature (6), and what Keats later (in *Ode to Psyche*) called the "working brain," which sees the same lightning as quite something else (29 ff.). The contrast might be thought to involve something very like Wordsworthian creative sensibility (cf. Wordsworth's *A whirl-blast from behind the hill,* where withered leaves, made to jump and spring by the pelting hailstones, are perceived as "Some Robin Good-fellow . . . dancing to the minstrelsy"), except that the imagination in Keats's poem attempts to communicate with a realm that "no mortal eye can reach" (44). The poetic "trance" is described as follows:

> But there are times, when those that love the bay,
> Fly from all sorrowing far, far away;
> A sudden glow comes on them, naught they see
> In water, earth, or air, but poesy. . . .
> [And] when a Poet is in such a trance,
> In air he sees white coursers paw, and prance,
> Bestridden of gay knights, in gay apparel,
> Who at each other tilt in playful quarrel,
> And what we, ignorantly, sheet-lightning call,

[10] They are briefly detailed in the first essay in the present volume.

Is the swift opening of their wide portal,
When the bright warder blows his trumpet clear,
Whose tones reach naught on earth but Poet's ear.
When these enchanted portals open wide,
And through the light the horsemen swiftly glide,
The Poet's eye can reach those golden halls,
And view the glory of their festivals. . . .
Yet further off, are dimly seen their bowers,
Of which, no mortal eye can reach the flowers;
And 'tis right just, for well Apollo knows
'Twould make the Poet quarrel with the rose. . . .

These wonders strange he sees, and many more,
Whose head is pregnant with poetic lore.   (19–54)

There are references to *seeing* ("see," "sees," "seen," "sight,"
"eye," and "view") in lines 21, 26, 35, 36, 43, 44, 53, 57, 63, 65,
and what is seen—"enchanted portals," "golden halls," "wonders
strange"—is not of this world.

Sleep and Poetry again has an early reference to visions (in
l. 10, where it is last, and therefore the most significant, in a
list of items associated with sleep). The central apostrophe to
Poesy contains "Visions of . . . elysium" (63–64, a Huntian
"bowery nook") as well as fireside imaginings, and subsequently
there is the vision of the charioteer and the fleeing of that vision,
which is replaced by "A sense of real things . . . like a muddy
stream . . . bear[ing] along / My soul to nothingness" (125–
159). The conventional poetic *flight* is suggested in the line
"Wings to find out an immortality" (84), and rendered literally
in the identification of imagination with the chariot ("freely fly
. . . prepare her steeds, / Paw up against the light, and do strange
deeds / Upon the clouds," 164–167). When Keats says that poetry
should "lift the thoughts of man" (247), one suspects a literal
elevation that we do not normally associate with "lift" (cf. "uplifted from the world" in *I stood tip-toe,* l. 139).

Keats never entirely relinquishes his interest in this basic idea

of the imagination's ability to mount up and penetrate to a
higher realm of reality. As I have suggested elsewhere in this
volume, it is a central issue in *Endymion,* which is a testing of
the truth or "authenticity" of what this kind of imagination finds
out; it figures prominently in Keats's letter of 22 November 1817
to Benjamin Bailey (the imagination is "a Shadow of reality to
come" and has an "empyreal reflection" that prefigures a "spiritual repetition" of human life);[11] and it appears in many of the
major poems of 1819, usually in the form of dreaming—so frequently, in fact, that the concern with visionary imagination may
be taken as Keats's central theme, in the same way that the naturalized imagination of creative sensibility may be taken as Wordsworth's. This does not, however, mean that we can call Keats a
visionary. As in a late Keats usage ("vision'ries . . . dreamers
weak" in *The Fall of Hyperion,* I.161–162), just as in our everyday use of the word, a "visionary" cannot cope with the practical
problems of life. The burden of Keats's poetry after *Endymion*
(and even in the ambiguities of that poem) is that the visionary
imagination does not "work"—in various poems either is not
authentic (a "fancy," a "cheat," a hoodwinking) or is impractical as a solution to human problems, since, by his very nature,
man cannot attain permanently the higher realms of nightingale,
urn, La Belle Dame's grot, or Lamia's palace. "Forlorn" brings
the speaker of *Ode to a Nightingale* back to his "sole self," and
back to earth, and visionary wings are traded for something more
substantial. "I have of late been moulting," Keats told J. H.
Reynolds on 11 July 1819, when he had just completed Part I
of *Lamia:* "not for fresh feathers & wings: they are gone, and
in their stead I hope to have a pair of patient sublunary legs.
I have altered, not from a Chrysalis into a butterfly, but the Contrary. having two little loopholes, whence I may look out into
the stage of the world" (*Letters,* II, 128).

[11] *The Letters of John Keats,* ed. Hyder E. Rollins (Cambridge, Mass.,
1958), I, 185. On the complexities of this letter, see Appendix I, below.

V

It has long been a challenge to put Wordsworth and Keats to-gether—the two best poets of the period—as a basis for defining "Romanticism." There are many connections between them: [12] they were acquaintances; Keats was a great admirer of Words-worth (and sometimes also a very perceptive critic of his literary and personal shortcomings); both delighted in nature and in "sensation"; both were interested in the condition of man in this world, and were aware of the pain and suffering inherent in man's mortal nature; both posited schemes of individual devel-opment by marked stages of ascent; and so on. As is well known, Wordsworth exerted a good deal of influence, both general and specific, on Keats's writings—for example, in the ideas of the function of poetry set down in the 1817 volume, the concept of the origin of myths in *I stood tip-toe* (based on Book IV of *The Excursion*), the humanitarian tendencies of *Sleep and Poetry* (as in the resolve to deal with "the agonies, the strife / Of human hearts"), the affirmation of "the holiness of the Heart's affec-tions" and the preference for a "Life of Sensations" in the letter to Bailey of 22 November 1817. And there are similarities in their works that represent not so much influence as a basic like-ness in their attitudes toward life, nature, and imagination. I have pointed out elsewhere that lines in Book VI of *The Prelude* (which Keats of course never read)—

> Our destiny, our being's heart and home,
> Is with infinitude, and only there;
> With hope it is, hope that can never die,

[12] On the relationships between them and the influence of the older on the younger poet, see, among others, Clarence D. Thorpe, "Wordsworth and Keats—A Study in Personal and Critical Impression," *PMLA,* XLII (1927), 1010–26; John Middleton Murry, *Keats* (London, 1955), pp. 269–291; Thora Balslev, *Keats and Wordsworth: A Comparative Study* (Copen-hagen, 1962).

> Effort, and expectation, and desire,
> And something evermore about to be   (604–608)

—say much the same thing as Keats in a letter to Bailey of 13
March 1818: "every mental pursuit takes its reality and worth
from the ardour of the pursuer—being in itself a nothing" (*Letters*, I, 242). *Peter Bell,* whose Prologue presents a literal flight
to the unworldly followed by a glad return to "the dear green
Earth"—the structure that I discussed in the essay on Keats's odes
—was published in April 1819, the month in which Keats wrote
the first of those odes. And a passage of Wordsworth's *Elegiac
Stanzas*—

> Farewell, farewell the heart that lives alone,
> Housed in a dream, at distance from the Kind!
> Such happiness, wherever it be known,
> Is to be pitied; for 'tis surely blind   (53–56)

—could serve as an epigraph to Keats's entire work.

What the two poets chiefly have in common is their idea of
the importance of imagination, which each, in different ways,
made the central concern of his work. It is the "different ways"
that has been the main obstacle to putting the two together.
Wordsworth deals with a down-to-earth imagination that operates within Locke's and Hartley's terms to perceive, and in perceiving transform, the natural world; Keats deals with a high-
flying imagination that violates Locke's and Hartley's terms and
that departs from the natural world in search of some supernatural realm. The one assumes a monistic view of the universe,
the other a dualistic view. At face value, the two types ought to
be unreconcilable.

The essential link between these two poets' writings about the
imagination lies in the ultimate purpose that they put imagination to, and the final attitudes they strike. Fundamentally, their
theories of imagination are theories of life. Wordsworth is
throughout interested in the question of the goodness of man,

whose mind was held to be a mechanism, a slave to the despotism of "the bodily eye." Discovering genuine creativity in his repeated explorations of the mind's activity, he arrives at "A more judicious knowledge of the worth / And dignity of individual man" (*The Prelude,* XIII.80–81). His celebration of imagination is a celebration of human nature: the mind of man is found capable of becoming "A thousand times more beautiful than the earth / On which he dwells" (XIV.449–450). Similarly Keats employs imagination as a basis, not for poetry, but for taking attitudes about life in the actual world. The desire to get out of the world, to attain some higher reality where the conditions of mortality do not prevail, is a renunciation of the actual world; and the "homeward fever" of his heroes, desperate to return to their native soil, is an affirmation of the superior worth of that same world. The fact is that Wordsworth's celebration of one kind of imagination and Keats's progressive skepticism about the "authenticity" of the other amount to a shared acceptance of the value for its own sake of human life in the transient natural world.

To return to some statements made at the beginning of this essay, Wordsworth of course did not really think that flowers enjoy the air they breathe, and Keats did not for a minute really think that a man could find a better life with a nightingale in a dark forest. Rather, they were concerned to explore the question of how man comes to terms with himself and his surroundings in a world in which flowers have no consciousness and nightingales, however sweetly they sing, are just ordinary birds after all. Wordsworth demonstrates that in certain circumstances a perceiver's creative imagination can transform the world, and that experiences of this kind of transformation (as, for example, in *Tintern Abbey, I wandered lonely as a cloud,* the "spots of time" in *The Prelude*) have long-lasting beneficial effects, both for the feelings and for the intellect. Keats produced dramas of displacement to show the various bad results of pursuing a false or impossibly ideal vision

of the sort that Wordsworth attributes to the early Coleridge in
Book VI of *The Prelude:*

> . . . Platonic forms
> Of wild ideal pageantry, shaped out
> From things well-matched or ill, and words for things,
> The self-created sustenance of a mind
> Debarred from Nature's living images,
> Compelled to be a life unto herself,
> And unrelentingly possessed by thirst
> Of greatness, love, and beauty.   (298–305)

Neither poet would deny that the "thirst / Of greatness, love,
and beauty" is a good thing, but both would hold that it can
be satisfied only in the real world in which they lived—"the
world / Of all of us,—the place where, in the end, / We find
our happiness, or not at all!" (*The Prelude,* XI.142–144). The
"Romanticism" of Wordsworth and Keats is ultimately an affirmation of mundane reality.

VI

To clear up the question of how a "Romanticism" can be an affirmation of reality, I should like in this final section to distinguish between two kinds of Romanticism on the basis of the
two kinds of imagination singled out above. In attempting to
remedy or compensate for the breakdown of unity and the limitations on man's creative faculties, the writers who invested in
the visionary imagination aimed toward a separation from the
actual world of flux, a transcending or going-beyond that involved a dualistic concept of the universe. The writers who pursued such transcendence are rightly (by the twentieth-century
humanists) called escapists and viewed as proposers of false or
impossible solutions that depend on one or another outdated
system of belief—Platonism, Christian dualism, various home-
made varieties of mysticism—that we no longer allow to be ten-
able. On the other hand, the writers who invested in what has

been described here as the naturalized imagination were intent not on escape but on a genuine union, a merging with the world, on some monistic basis. The remedies proposed by these writers are "true" solutions, because, rather than invoking some outdated religious or philosophic system, they dealt with problems in terms of up-to-date, even acceptably "modern," ideas of the nature of the physical world and the workings of the human mind. To make the simplest kind of distinction on the basis of their compatibility with twentieth-century ways of thinking, the visionaries are the "false" or archaic Romantics, while the naturalizers are the "true" or modern.

Wallace Stevens seems to make a similarly simple and basic discrimination in the various comments on "the romantic" in his prose.[13] In an essay on "Imagination as Value" he speaks of "the difference between the imagination as metaphysics and as a power of the mind over external objects, that is to say, reality." He quotes a comment by Ernst Cassirer on the "universal metaphysical value" of imagination, and says that Cassirer is talking about "romantic thought"—"and by romantic thought [Cassirer] means metaphysics." A page and a half later Stevens urges that "we must somehow cleanse the imagination of the romantic. . . . The imagination is one of the great human powers. The romantic belittles it. . . . The imagination is the only genius. It is intrepid and eager and the extreme of its achievement lies in abstraction. The achievement of the romantic, on the contrary, lies in minor

---

[13] Although I arrived at the distinction between "false" and "true" Romanticism several years ago, for my use of Stevens in this and the next paragraphs I am initially indebted to a review by Joseph N. Riddel in *Journal of English and Germanic Philology,* LXVIII (1969), 718–723, which mentions "what Stevens calls two kinds of Romanticism: the one false, clutching nostalgically to a metaphysical source, long since disproven, which supplies the imagination with vatic powers; the other true, and ever-present in the continuous struggle of subject and object," and to some suggestions that Riddel sent me in correspondence afterward.

wish-fulfillments and it is incapable of abstraction." [14] The basic
distinction is clear enough. There are two kinds of imagination,
and one of them, the "romantic," which is identifiable with the
visionary imagination of the present essay ("imagination as metaphysics," "minor wish-fulfillments"), is condemned ("we must
somehow cleanse" it). The other kind is "the only genius," an
imagination that comes to terms with reality.

Stevens does not associate the "true" imagination with Romanticism in the essay just cited, but he does so in two earlier pieces
included in *Opus Posthumous*. Reviewing Marianne Moore's
Selected Poems in *Life and Letters Today* (1935), he says that
her poems "clearly . . . are romantic": "At this point one very
well might stop for definitions. It is clear enough . . . to say
that the romantic in the pejorative sense merely connotes obsolescence, but that the word has, or should have, another sense.
. . . the romantic in its other sense, meaning always the living
and at the same time the imaginative, the youthful, the delicate
and a variety of [other] things . . . constitutes the vital element
in poetry." As the "most brilliant instance of the romantic in this
sense," Stevens names T. S. Eliot, "who incessantly revives the
past and creates the future. It is a process of cross-fertilization,
an immense process . . . of hybridization." And, quoting Miss
Moore's famous line, "imaginary gardens with real toads in
them," he comments, "The very conjunction of imaginary gardens and real toads is one more specimen of the romantic." [15]
The other relevant piece is his Preface to William Carlos Williams' *Collected Poems, 1921–1931* (1934), in which he declares
that Williams "is a romantic poet," and then goes on to explain,
pretty much in the way he characterizes the poetry of Miss Moore
and Eliot:

[14] *The Necessary Angel: Essays on Reality and the Imagination* (New
York, 1951), pp. 136–139.
[15] *Opus Posthumous* (New York, 1957), pp. 251–253.

. . . the essential poetry is the result of the conjunction of the unreal and the real, the sentimental and the anti-poetic, the constant inter-action of two opposites. . . .

All poets are, to some extent, romantic poets. . . . What, then, is a romantic poet now-a-days? He happens to be one who still dwells in an ivory tower, but who insists that life would be intolerable except for the fact that one has, from the top, such an exceptional view of the public dump and the advertising signs of Snider's Catsup, Ivory Soap and Chevrolet Cars; he is the hermit who dwells alone with the sun and moon, but insists on taking a rotten newspaper.[16]

In these extracts, the "other sense" of "romantic," which involves the conjunction (cross-fertilization, hybridization, interaction) of the unreal and the real, is what I have been trying to describe in the theory and practice of Wordsworth and Keats. As opposed to the Romanticism of "obsolescence" (by now virtually obso-lete), this is a modern Romanticism, and it represents the con-tinuity in "the essential poetry" from Wordsworth and Keats to the present day.

The constant dilemma facing the modern writer (and at this point I wish to include Wordsworth and Keats in a concept that sees "modern" literature as nearly two centuries old) is how to transcend a kind of literal things-as-they-are realism when there is no longer any agreed-on system of belief that allows for such transcendence. (Wordsworth as a modern poet had "No little band of yet remembered names / Whom I, in perfect confidence, might hope / To summon back from lonesome banishment," he says in The Prelude, I.161–163; it was, as he feared in Peter Bell, l. 127, "an age too late." Keats as a modern poet had the same perception in Ode to Psyche, ll. 37–41: the present was for him an age "too late for the fond believing lyre, / When holy were the haunted forest boughs, / Holy the air, the water, and the fire," an age "so far retir'd / From happy pieties.") I would suggest that Wordsworth and Keats, just as much as Stevens,

[16] Opus Posthumous, pp. 254–256.

Williams, and other important poets of the twentieth century, did manage to achieve both realism and a kind of transcendence via imagination without depending on any such outdated system. Wordsworth *spiritualizes* ordinary objects and incidents so as to make them new and strange—in Coleridge's words, gives "the charm of novelty to things of every day, and . . . excite[s] a feeling *analogous to the supernatural,* by awakening the mind's attention from the lethargy of custom, and directing it to the loveliness and the wonders of the world before us" (*Biographia Literaria,* ch. XIV, italics mine)—and he does this without violating the toughest laws of common-sense realism. Keats attempts to transcendentalize, and in his major poems fails, but is reconciled to the failure and to the real world that he has remaining. In their mental excursions his characters see "wonders strange," but in the end they come back to earth. In both poets, the imagination operates to produce "something more," but does so without cheating. Stevens and Williams were well aware that "our perishing earth" was "all of paradise that we shall know." [17] It is the same perishing earth that the earliest modern Romantics, Wordsworth and Keats, ultimately placed their faith in.

[17] Stevens' *Sunday Morning,* ll. 79, 41.

Appendix I:
Keats's Letter to Bailey on the Imagination

In several of the essays in the present volume I have referred to Keats's letter to Benjamin Bailey of 22 November 1817 (*Letters,* I, 183–187), and made a point on the basis of the passages that in recent years have seemed the most important to critics—Keats's affirmation of "the authenticity of the Imagination" and his comparison of the imagination with Adam's dream, "he awoke and found it truth." For the sake of expediency, and to keep the focus on concerns of the poems, I have, like most other critics, ignored a number of complications in that letter. These may, however, in the space of an appendix, be briefly discussed as a caution to anyone who thinks that in November 1817 Keats's mind was clear on the subject.[1]

The general background for the topic of "the authenticity of the Imagination" is the epistemological and psychological dilemma concerning imagination and creativity posed most bluntly by Locke and his followers in the eighteenth century, and the

---

[1] The letter has been frequently discussed. See Walter H. Evert, *Aesthetic and Myth in the Poetry of Keats* (Princeton, 1965), pp. 284–285 n., for the principal references. James Ralston Caldwell, *John Keats' Fancy* (Ithaca, 1945), pp. 100–102, 134–135, 153–158, and Newell F. Ford, *The Prefigurative Imagination of John Keats* (Stanford, 1951), pp. 20–38, are most aware of the complexities, though Caldwell does not explicate the letter in detail, and Ford finds only one sentence ("But as I was saying . . . that delicious face you will see") to be in contradiction with the rest. For a background in Bailey's own thinking, see Earl R. Wasserman, "Keats and Benjamin Bailey on the Imagination," *Modern Language Notes,* LXVIII (1953), 361–365.

two basic tendencies of the Romantics—by means of the naturalized imagination and the visionary imagination—to answer the
problem.[2] The more immediate background might well be Keats's
and Bailey's discussions of Wordsworth and Coleridge at Oxford
in September 1817. It is even possible to take their concern over
imagination (for both were concerned, Bailey experiencing a
"momentary start") as a worry stimulated specifically by *Biographia Literaria,* which was published in July 1817, and to see
Keats's letter as an attempt to counter Coleridge's statements
about the naturalized imagination in chapters XIII and XIV.[3]
Actually, however, the letter to Bailey embodies *both* the naturalized and visionary tendencies mentioned above. In the sentences on imagination Keats goes back and forth from a Locke-
Hartleian associationalism to a kind of higher-realms Platonism,
and he does not resolve the contradictions.

The important passage in question begins with an announce-
ment of the topic—"O I wish I was as certain of the end of all
your troubles as that of your momentary start about the authenticity of the Imagination"—and with an affirmation: "I am certain
of nothing but of the holiness of the Heart's affections and the
truth of Imagination." The phrase "holiness of the Heart's affections" has (since it contains three of Wordsworth's favorite words)
a Wordsworthian sound—one thinks of "that serene and blessed
mood, / In which the affections [= feelings, emotions resulting
from some influence] gently lead us on . . ." in *Tintern Abbey,*
lines 41–42, a poem that, like Keats's letter, opposes "sensations"
and "thoughts." When Keats speaks of "the truth of Imagination" he may at this point be thinking of almost anything, in-

[2] See "Keats, Wordsworth, and 'Romanticism,' " sections II–IV, above.
[3] When, a month later (27[?] December 1817), Keats chooses Coleridge
to exemplify the lack of Negative Capability—"Coleridge . . . would let
go by a fine isolated verisimilitude caught from the Penetralium of mystery,
from being incapable of remaining content with half knowledge" (*Letters,*
I, 193–194)—he is surely thinking of *Biographia Literaria.*

cluding the seeing "into the life of things" (49) that the affections lead to in Wordsworth's poem.

Keats next says that "What the imagination seizes as Beauty must be truth—whether it existed before or not—for I have the same Idea of all our Passions as of Love they are all in their sublime, creative of essential Beauty." This is a statement that the products of imagination are "real" whether discovered or created.[4] The phrase "whether it existed before or not" is usually taken as one element that defines the imagination as *prefigurative,* "foreshadowing . . . subsequent, substantial reality,"[5] as in Adam's dream when it is referred to a second time in the letter. One may note, however, that the phrase applies equally well to Wordsworthian creative sensibility, the results of which are also "true" whether they existed before or not. And there is, of course, much in Wordsworth on the creativity of the passions—for example, "the strong creative power / Of human passion" in *The Excursion,* I.480–481. It may be that the ideas of seizing and creating in Keats's sentence correspond to the perceiving and half-creating of *Tintern Abbey,* lines 106–107.

To document his statements, Keats refers to two passages of *Endymion:* "In a Word, you may know my favorite Speculation by my first Book and the little song I sent in my last—which is a representation from the fancy of the probable mode of operating in these Matters." This is a curious combination: Book I of *Endymion* is centrally about the authenticity of the *visionary* imagination, while "the little song"—the Indian maiden's "O Sorrow" in Book IV, lines 146–181—is about the creativity of

---

[4] The burden of the extracts from Hobbes through Priestley given in "Keats, Wordsworth, and 'Romanticism,'" section II, is that the truth "existed before."

[5] Ford, p. 26. In *Paradise Lost* it is not entirely clear that Adam's dream of the creation of Eve (VIII.452–490) is prefigurative, but after an earlier dream in the same book Adam "waked, and found / Before mine eyes all real, as the dream / Had lively shadowed" (309–311).

passion (Sorrow borrows color, light, sound, and feeling from some things in the natural and human world and gives them to others, an obvious instance of emotion affecting perception). Both passages of *Endymion* deal with "truth," but in the first (Book I) it "existed before" (as it turns out) and in the second ("O Sorrow") it did not. Though they are supposed to illustrate the same thing, they are actually more opposed than united, the one compatible with the visionary tendency, the other an example of the naturalized imagination. Keats seems to clear up the opposition in his next sentence, "The Imagination may be compared to Adam's dream—he awoke and found it truth," for there is no imaginative creating here but rather the authentic prefiguring of reality to come (as Keats's reference to "Adam's dream" a few sentences later makes clear).

The next several sentences discuss consecutive reasoning, truth, sensations, thoughts, and reality to come.

I am the more zealous in this affair, because I have never yet been able to perceive how any thing can be known for truth by consequitive reasoning—and yet it must be—Can it be that even the greatest Philosopher ever arrived at his goal without putting aside numerous objections—However it may be, O for a Life of Sensations rather than of Thoughts! It is 'a Vision in the form of Youth' a Shadow of reality to come—and this consideration has further conv[i]nced me for it has come as auxiliary to another favorite Speculation of mine, that we shall enjoy ourselves here after by having what we called happiness on Earth repeated in a finer tone and so repeated—And yet such a fate can only befall those who delight in sensation rather than hunger as you do after Truth—Adam's dream will do here and seems to be a conviction that Imagination and its empyreal reflection is the same as human Life and its spiritual repetition.

It is obvious that sensation (rather than thought, consecutive reasoning, hungering after truth) is important to imagination, at least to the "simple imaginative Mind." But what kind of imagination is being talked about? The opposition of "Sensations"

and "Thoughts" again suggests an opting for the heart's affections and the creativity of the passions that I have referred to
in Wordsworth. "Shadow of reality to come," "enjoy ourselves
here after," and "spiritual repetition" all suggest, however, that
Keats is still—or once more—thinking of the prefigurative or
visionary imagination. One can explain the three phrases in terms
of Wordsworthian creative sensibility. In the process of association, stored up impressions do, in a sense, provide a "reality to
come" (Coleridge laments the loss of such a reality in the opening of *This Lime-Tree Bower My Prison*—"I have lost / Beauties
and feelings, such as would have been / Most sweet to my re-
membrance even when age / Had dimm'd mine eyes to blind-
ness!"). "Enjoy ourselves here after" may refer to a future time
on earth, and in recollection there is a refining process that might
be described in the phrase "repeated in a finer tone." "Spiritual
repetition" can easily be taken as "mental repetition" rather than
"repetition in a spiritual or non-physical world" ("spiritual" and
"mental," like "soul" and "mind," are virtually synonymous in
Wordsworth). The last sentence extracted above, however, seems
to tip the balance toward the visionary again. Some parallels are
set up: imagination is related to an empyreal (heavenly) reflection (counterpart) just as human life is related to a spiritual or
mental counterpart; or, to reverse the order of Keats's phrases,
just as the reality of human life has a counterpart in mental reality, so the imagination has a counterpart in another world. There
is no getting around the implications of "empyreal," which plainly
assumes another realm of existence.

See what follows, however. Keats seems to resume after a
pause—

But as I was saying—the simple imaginative Mind may have its re-
wards in the repeti[ti]on of its own silent Working coming continually
on the spirit with a fine suddenness—to compare great things with
small—have you never by being surprised with an old Melody—in a
delicious place—by a delicious voice, fe[l]t over again your very specu-

lations and surmises at the time it first operated on your soul—do you not remember forming to you[r]self the singer's face more beautiful that [for than] it was possible and yet with the elevation of the Moment you did not think so. . . .

The passage uses the same terms as the preceding—"imaginative," "repetition," "spirit"—but is clearly talking about the process of association: an old melody triggers various recollections (the first hearing of the melody, the listener's circumstances at the time), and they are repeated in "a finer tone" ("more beautiful," "elevation of the Moment").[6] On this example, "spiritual repetition" must be given the down-to-earth interpretation ("mental repetition") that I suggested in the preceding paragraph. But then Keats continues the last sentence, ". . . even then you were mounted on the Wings of Imagination so high—that the Prototype must be here after—that delicious face you will see." And with this "mount[ing] on . . . Wings" and "Prototype . . . here after" Keats has returned to his visionary or prefigurative notion.

Thus in the space of about a page Keats has talked about affections, imagination, beauty, truth, creativity, Adam's dream, sensations, thoughts, happiness on earth, spiritual repetition, recollection of music, and the future seeing of a prototype. About half of his statements can be aligned with the naturalizing tendency mentioned at the beginning, an idea of imagination that works in and on the real world, and does so within Locke's and Hartley's concept of the way the mind functions; the other half of his statements can be interpreted in terms of the visionary tendency in which the imagination penetrates to a higher reality. A number of the statements, and some of the most important, can be interpreted *both* ways at once. I think it is still fair, and also useful, to extract the idea of the "authenticity" or "truth" of imagination, and the example of Adam's dream, and connect them with the main topic of *Endymion* in Books I and IV (the "authenticity"

[6] See Caldwell, pp. 101–102, for examples of association based on music in James Beattie and Archibald Alison.

of Endymion's dreams) and with the questioning of visionary experiences in the poems of 1819. But it is well to recognize that it
was not only in *Endymion* that Keats's mind was, as he told
Shelley three years later, "like a pack of scattered cards" (*Letters,*
II, 323). The letter to Bailey is a fascinating and valuable—and
also very mixed-up—piece of prose.

Appendix II:
The Text of
The Eve of St. Agnes

The first edition of H. W. Garrod's *The Poetical Works of John Keats* (Oxford, 1939) was published with some 135 errors and omissions[1] in the *apparatus criticus* to *The Eve of St. Agnes*. About twenty substantive variants were left unrecorded, and there were some forty misprints and mistakes in transcription, thirty-five instances of wrong or incomplete sigla, and forty other errors in description of the various manuscripts underlying the printed text. While it might be supposed that some of these would have been corrected in the second edition (1958), the fact is that not a single remedial change was introduced. But there is a more worrisome matter concerning the soundness of the text itself—not only Garrod's but all printed texts of Keats's poem—a matter that depends not so much on a rechecking of the manuscripts (for the facts surrounding the text have for some time been available) as on an editor's judgment. At least since the publication of Amy Lowell's biography (1925) it has been known that Keats's publishers enforced changes in the language of the poem; but so far no editor has attempted to repair Keats's text or in any way depart from the version first printed, in the *Lamia* volume of 1820.

Keats first drafted the poem during the last two weeks of Janu-

---

[1] This and the following figures (which do not, of course, include the omission of several hundred accidental variants among the manuscripts) are slightly understated to allow for disagreement in a few questionable readings. I am not here primarily concerned with Garrod's errors, which, amid a wealth of valuable detail, are relatively unimportant.

ary (and perhaps also the first week or so of February) 1819. His original manuscript (Garrod's *H,* now in the Harvard Keats Collection) was twice copied by Richard Woodhouse, legal and literary adviser to Keats's publishers, in the transcripts designated by Garrod as W^1 and W^2 (both are at Harvard). The evidence for the order of these independent copies is ambiguous, but W^1, showing a few more errors and more blank spaces where Keats's manuscript could not be read, would seem to be the earlier; W^2 is dated by Woodhouse 20 April 1819. Early in September Keats revised the poem and had it "copied fair" (*Letters,* II, 157, 162). His fair copy, presumably the one sent to the publishers, is now lost, but in the following January, perhaps on the 15th (see *Letters,* II, 243), George Keats copied it in the transcript known as *E* (British Museum), and sometime before or afterward—probably both [2]—Woodhouse read it and entered corrections and variant readings (designated *w* by Garrod) between the lines and opposite the text of W^2. "The agreement . . . of *E* and *w,*" writes Garrod (2nd ed., p. xli), disregarding the question of variants between them, and actually intending to include the agreement of *E* with the other manuscripts as well, "represents Keats' fair copy. . . . Any divergence of *1820* from *Ew* must be interpreted as a change made in proof either by Keats himself or by his publishers." Not counting copyist's errors, there are more than forty such substantive "divergences"; it is a nice question, in each instance, whether Keats or his publishers were responsible.

Concerning a few of them, however, I think it is time we reached a decision. On 12 September 1819 Keats read the revised form of the poem to Woodhouse, who gave the following report to the publisher John Taylor in a letter of 19 September:

---

[2] Again the evidence is ambiguous, for while *E* and *w* usually show the same revised readings, there are still several instances of disagreement between them in which 1820 agrees sometimes with *E,* sometimes with *w,* occasionally with neither. The readiest explanation would seem to be that Woodhouse entered the *w* readings at various times, perhaps some of them even after the poem was printed.

[Keats] had the Eve of St A. copied fair: He has made trifling alterations, inserted an additional stanza early in the poem to make the
legend more intelligible, and correspondent with what afterwards takes
place, particularly with respect to the supper & the playing on the
Lute.—he retains the name of Porphyro—has altered the last 3 lines
to leave on the reader a sense of pettish disgust, by bringing Old
Angela in (only) dead stiff & ugly. . . . There was another alteration,
which I abused for "a full hour by the *Temple* clock." You know if a
thing has a decent side, I generally look no further—As the Poem was
orig^y written, *we* innocent ones (ladies & myself) might very well have
supposed that Porphyro, when acquainted with Madeline's love for
him, & when "he arose, Etherial flush^d &c &c (turn to it) set himself at
once to persuade her to go off with him, & succeeded & went over the
"Dartmoor black" (now changed for some other place) to be married,
in right honest chaste & sober wise. But, as it is now altered, as soon
as M. has confessed her love, P. winds by degrees his arm round her,
presses breast to breast, and acts all the acts of a bonâ fide husband,
while she fancies she is only playing the part of a Wife in a dream.
This alteration is of about 3 stanzas; and tho' there are no improper
expressions but all is left to inference, and tho' profanely speaking, the
Interest on the reader's imagination is greatly heightened, yet I do
apprehend it will render the poem unfit for ladies, & indeed scarcely
to be mentioned to them among the "things that are." (*Letters*, II,
162–163)

Of the three revisions here specified (apart from the change
of the hero's name), only one should cause us difficulty, the alteration of the last three lines. In all extant versions, from the first
draft on, Angela is brought in (in a sense) "dead stiff & ugly,"
and always accompanied by the Beadsman, whose death is a
similarly grotesque affair. In HW^1W^2 and the 1820 text, "meagre
face deform" describes Angela; through a change in punctuation
the corresponding phrase in *Ew* ("with face deform") is made to
apply to the Beadsman. But in no extant version is Angela "only"
introduced. One could suppose a lost ending, but I rather think
that Woodhouse, who had heard the revised version but obviously

had not yet read it, and who, furthermore, had been given plenty to think about by one of the earlier alterations that he describes, simply misunderstood the revised ending. In any event, the alteration (of whatever nature) has no place in the final text of the poem: beneath the variant ending (*w*) in W^2 Woodhouse wrote "Altered 1820." and two words in shorthand that are best read as "before March." [3] Presumably, before March 1820, when he was preparing his poems for publication, Keats restored the original conclusion of the poem.

The other two alterations are a simpler matter. The "additional stanza" inserted "early in the poem" is of course that given in the *Ew* transcripts between the present stanzas VI and VII:

> 'Twas said her future lord would there appear
> Offering, as sacrifice—all in the dream—
> Delicious food, even to her lips brought near,
> Viands, and wine, and fruit, and sugar'd cream,
> To touch her palate with the fine extreme
> Of relish: then soft music heard, and then
> More pleasures [4] follow'd in a dizzy stream
> Palpable almost: then to wake again
> Warm in the virgin morn, no weeping Magdalen. [5]

---

[3] I am indebted to the late Mabel A. E. Steele, former Curator of the Harvard Keats Collection, who told me that the shorthand notations seem to have been written hastily: "the second word is almost certainly 'March,' and, if we accept that reading, the first is *probably* 'before.' It breaks down into 'b,' the first part of either 'f' or 'x,' and what ought to be 'l,' because the stroke seems to go down. If it went up from the loop, stopping at the top, it would be 'r.' "

[4] So *Ew;* Garrod's "pleasure" (2nd ed. only) is a misprint.

[5] I quote the *w* version as the one more likely to represent the minutiae of Keats's lost copy accurately; the *E* transcript (reproduced in most respects faithfully by Garrod, 1958, p. 238) shows nine variants in punctuation and spelling. In *w* the stanza is numbered "7"; with the "corrected Copy" before him Woodhouse struck through the original fourth stanza (see Garrod, p. 237) and renumbered the next three stanzas "4," "5," and "6." In *E*, and presumably therefore in Keats's lost fair copy, all the stanzas were unnumbered.

The alteration that Woodhouse "abused for 'a full hour by the *Temple* clock'" was a revision of the present lines 314–322 to read:

> See, while she speaks his arms encroaching slow,
> Have zoned her, heart to heart,—loud, loud the dark winds blow!
>
> For on the midnight came a tempest fell;
> More sooth, for that his quick rejoinder flows
> Into her burning ear: and still the spell
> Unbroken guards her in serene repose.
> With her wild dream he mingled, as a rose
> Marrieth its odour to a violet.
> Still, still she dreams, louder the frost wind blows.[6]

Because Woodhouse calls it an "alteration . . . of about 3 stanzas," Lowell, Garrod, and others have felt that the revised version to which he objected has been lost. But the lines just quoted fit all the other details of Woodhouse's description ("winds by degrees his arm round her, presses breast to breast, and acts all the acts of a bonâ fide husband, while she fancies she is only playing the part of a Wife in a dream. . . . there are no improper expressions but all is left to inference"). Woodhouse wrote *"about* 3 stanzas"; the revised lines affect two stanzas. If we again recall that Woodhouse had heard, not read, the poem when he wrote to Taylor, and also consider that the revised text, by setting off a train of uncomfortable thoughts in his mind, quite possibly would have seemed longer than it really was, it should become plain that the *Ew* lines we now possess are those that Woodhouse was afraid would make the poem "unfit for ladies."

In his reply to Woodhouse of 25 September, Taylor confessed that the account of this last revision excited in him "the Strongest

[6] Again I transcribe the *w* text; the *E* version (followed except in three marks of punctuation by Garrod, p. 252) shows eleven variants in punctuation and spelling, and has (as Garrod indicates) "close" for "quick" in the second line of the new stanza. In both *E* and *w* the last line quoted here ends with a comma.

Sentiments of Disapprobation," and he added: "Therefore my dear Rich^d if [Keats] will not so far concede to my Wishes as to leave the passage as it originally stood, I must be content to admire his Poems with some other Imprint" (*Letters,* II, 183). Obviously the publishers forced the restoration of the original lines 314–322, and it is almost as certain that they forced the rejection of the additional stanza inserted between VI and VII. Once the possibility of sexual references had been opened, the lines describing "More pleasures . . . in a dizzy stream," "virgin morn," and "weeping Magdalen" (very likely an allusion to the deserted unwed mother of Book VI of *The Excursion,* who is called "a weeping Magdalene" and "a rueful Magdalene" in ll. 814, 987) would similarly have rendered the poem, by the publishers' standard, "unfit for ladies."

Just as clearly, the revised lines and the additional stanza should be restored *to the text* of the poem. In "The Hoodwinking of Madeline" (above in the present volume) I have suggested ways in which these passages heighten the irony of Madeline's self-deception and clarify Keats's condemnation of "dreaming" (Madeline's engrossment in superstitious ritual to the point of losing touch with reality). More relevant here is Keats's recoverable intention in the matter of text. On the one hand, we know that he vigorously opposed Woodhouse's objections: "He says," Woodhouse noted in the same report to Taylor, "he does not want ladies to read his poetry: that he writes for men—& that if in the former poem [i.e., the original version of the consummation] there was an opening for doubt what took place, it was his fault for not writing clearly & comprehensibly—that he sh^d despise a man who would be such an eunuch in sentiment as to leave a maid, with that Character about her, in such a situation: & sho^d despise himself to write about it &c &c &c—and all this sort of Keats-like rhodomontade" (*Letters,* II, 163). On the other hand, to balance this, we have only Woodhouse's cryptic note in W^2 that "K. left it to his Publishers to adopt which [alterations] they pleased, & to revise the Whole." One can imagine with what willingness (and in what tone of voice) Keats surrendered that privilege.

Since an editor must always act according to principles, the problem facing an editor of Keats's poem is what, if he includes the *Ew* revisions so far discussed, he should do about the rest of the late manuscript readings that were rejected in 1820. A single example will serve to illustrate. In all extant transcripts the poem is called "Saint Agnes' [*or* Agnes] Eve" (Garrod's first textual note is wrong), which was always Keats's form of the title in his letters (see *Letters,* II, 58, 62, 139, 157, 174, 234, 294; so also Charles Brown, II, 276). Woodhouse and Taylor use forms of the title "The Eve of St. Agnes" (*Letters,* II, 162, 182), which appeared at the beginning of the poem, in the running heads, and on the title page and a half-title in the 1820 volume. Can we assume, then, that Keats's publishers altered the title? There is a strong possibility that they did. Can we assume, if they did, that Keats disapproved of the change? No—because we know that he read proofs of the poem, and that in at least two instances he insisted that his manuscript readings be restored (see *Letters,* II, 294–295). We can, I think, assume that he had a free hand wherever the publishers did not object specifically on moral or religious grounds.[7]

To only three other readings could the publishers have objected on such grounds. (1) At line 98, for "Mercy, Porphyro!" the manuscripts (some of them without the comma) read "Mercy, Jesu!"—which, aside from being metrically preferable, lends force to Angela's suspicions (detailed in stanza XIV) that the Porphyro confronting her may be an evil spirit. (2) At line 143, again in Angela's speech, for "Go, go!" the manuscripts (with minor variations) read "O Christ!"—a natural enough reaction just after

---

[7] The intense evangelicalism of Keats's otherwise amiable and worthy publishers is well illustrated in their letters written to Joseph Severn at Rome while Keats lay dying (see Hyder E. Rollins, *More Letters and Poems of the Keats Circle,* Cambridge, Mass., 1955, pp. 109–118).

the "cruel . . . impious . . . wicked" Porphyro has proposed his "stratagem." (3) At lines 145–147, for

> "I will not harm her, by all saints I swear,"
> Quoth Porphyro: "O may I ne'er find grace
> "When my weak voice shall whisper its last prayer . . ."

the manuscripts (with minor variations) read

> "I will not harm her, by the great Saint Paul—"
> Swear'th Porphyro—"O may I neer find grace
> "When my weak voice shall unto heaven call . . ."

—which, owing to Paul's association with chastity, embodies an ironic oath especially appropriate to Porphyro's plot against Madeline, but would have aroused the same disapproval from the publishers as the sexual overtones of the additional stanza between VI and VII.

The nearly forty other late manuscript readings that were ignored or rejected in 1820 have nothing in them offensive from a moral or religious point of view. The alterations are primarily stylistic, and in every instance we cannot be sure that Keats himself did not make the change in proof, or at least concur in the change if it was made by someone else. It is this circumstance that prevents us from always accepting the *Ew* agreement as Keat's final text: he *could* have been responsible for every single one of the stylistic alterations, from the title on.

Employing the principle that a proper text of the poem will embody the latest readings intended by the poet, including those that there is good reason to think were rejected by the publishers against the poet's wishes, future editors of Keats's poem, whether making an elaborate scholarly text or putting together selections for an anthology, should restore the *Ew* version of lines 314–322 and the additional stanza between VI and VII—this last even though it will result in the subsequent renumbering of stanzas and lines through most of the poem. Editors may wish to restore the manuscript readings at lines 98, 143, and 145–147; at present, while I myself favor them, these seem more a matter of individual option. Otherwise (saving for the need to tidy up the *apparatus criticus* in the next Oxford edition) the text we now have will serve.

Keats at one time thought enough of *The Eve of St. Agnes* to request that it appear first among the poems in the 1820 volume (*Letters,* II, 276). It seems less than fair not to accord it the best text possible; certainly the only slightly more innocent version we have always had, whether or not fit for ladies, has been often enough misunderstood.

Appendix III:
Who Says What
to Whom at the End of
Ode on a Grecian Urn?

I

Interpretation of the final lines of *Ode on a Grecian Urn* has frequently turned on the specific questions of who speaks the last thirteen words, and to whom. The textual evidence is inconclusive; each of the following versions has a claim to authority:

> Beauty is Truth,—Truth Beauty,—that is all
> Ye know on earth, and all ye need to know.
> (consensus of four transcripts; capitalization varies)

> Beauty is Truth, Truth Beauty.—That is all
> Ye know on Earth, and all ye need to know.
> (*Annals of the Fine Arts, for MDCCCXIX*)

> "Beauty is truth, truth beauty,"—that is all
> Ye know on earth, and all ye need to know.
> (Keats's *Lamia* volume)

Scholars have sometimes taken the consensus of punctuation in the four extant transcripts—by Charles Brown (Harvard), Richard Woodhouse (Harvard), George Keats (British Museum), and Charles Dilke (Keats House, Hampstead)—as strong evidence that Keats meant the urn to speak all of the last two lines.[1] As a critical exercise, each reader may decide for himself whether the division of these lines by dashes into three parts, even if Keats

---

[1] E.g., Alvin Whitley, "The Message of the Grecian Urn," *Keats-Shelley Memorial Bulletin*, No. 5 (1953), pp. 1–3; Jacob D. Wigod, "Keats's Ideal in the *Ode on a Grecian Urn*," *PMLA*, LXXII (1957), 118 n.

himself made the division, amounts to any clear indication of the poet's intention in the matter. In the logic of textual scholarship, however, the question is beside the point, for the agreement of the transcripts does not necessarily show that Keats ever punctuated the lines in the same way. (There is no extant version in Keats's handwriting, though some critics persist in quoting one.)

The validity of citing the four transcripts as evidence depends on the knowledge (1) that each transcriber made his copy directly from a Keats holograph; (2) that any transcript made from a Keats holograph faithfully reproduced its punctuation; (3) that no different version strongly contests the transcripts' reading for authority (i.e., that a holograph copied represents Keats's intention better than any other version that he may have been responsible for). No such knowledge can be established. Woodhouse copied Brown's version, not Keats's, as he indicated by adding "from C.B." at the end of his transcript. George Keats made his copy when he returned briefly to England in January 1820, some eight months after the poem was written. The first page of the notebook containing his transcript bears the inscription "George Keats. 1820," and on 15 January 1820 Keats wrote that "George is busy this morning in making copies of my verses" (*Letters,* II, 243). It cannot be shown that George copied Keats's manuscript rather than, say, Brown's presumably more readable transcript. Nothing is known of the circumstances behind the transcript made by Dilke, who moved away from Hampstead before the poem was written. It *is* likely that Brown copied directly from Keats's manuscript (and did so before the poem was printed), but the possibility that his was the only firsthand transcript is just as strong as the possibility that there was a plurality of such copies. The agreement of the four transcripts is, then, not very significant, considering the lack of facts about them.

No one has reported on the abilities and peculiarities of the transcribers in question. The most scholarly of them, Woodhouse, is disqualified here because he did not follow Keats's manuscript directly. As the one most likely to have copied Keats, Brown especially should be tested, but which extant Brown transcripts were made from which extant Keats holographs has never been determined. One available example, though not a very satisfactory one, is Keats's letter of 30 (dated 28) September 1820, in which, many years later when he copied it into his manuscript "Life of John Keats," Brown made forty-seven additions and changes in punctuation.[2] Keats's holograph and Brown's transcript of *Lines on the Mermaid Tavern* in the Harvard Keats Collection may briefly illustrate the general problem of the reliability of transcripts, regardless of whether the holograph is the original draft or whether it is the one that Brown copied. A comparison of the two shows seventeen additions and variants in punctuation in Brown's transcript. If one assumes (for the sake of argument) that the holograph uniquely represents Keats's approved form of the poem—it is the same kind of assumption that citing four transcripts of *Ode on a Grecian Urn* makes—then, if the holograph had been lost, we would be clearly wrong in attributing to Keats every mark of punctuation in Brown's transcript. Reliance on Brown's copy of *Ode on a Grecian Urn* is liable to the possibility of similar error.

Against the transcripts' three-part division of the lines stand the two original printed versions, which set off "Beauty is truth, truth beauty" as a unit by itself. The first appeared in James Elmes's *Annals of the Fine Arts, for MDCCCXIX* (published ca. January 1820). Its authority is sometimes discounted on the ground that B. R. Haydon, as he recalled in 1845, "begged a copy [of the *Nightingale* and *Grecian Urn* odes] for the Annals . . . and there they appeared at my request before the[y] came out in a Volume" (*Keats Circle,* II, 142). But Haydon's words can hardly be taken to mean that *he* transcribed the version for Elmes. As a matter of fact, in June 1819 Keats himself copied and sent to Elmes some

---

[2] Compare *Letters,* II, 344–346, and *The Keats Circle,* ed. Hyder E. Rollins (Cambridge, Mass., 1948), II, 80–82.

"verses" (*Letters,* II, 118–119, 120)—presumably *Ode to a Nightingale,* which appeared in the *Annals* in July. Although Haydon later noted that the *Annals* text of *Ode on a Grecian Urn* was "sent by me,"[3] there is no reason to suppose that Keats did not make the copy, just as he had with the other poem.

The other early printing is in the *Lamia* volume, published around 1 July 1820. This text is often denied authority on the ground that Keats was too ill to supervise publication, and the idea gains some support from Woodhouse's draft of an "Advertisement" to *Lamia,* in which he says that "the Author's health is not at pres[t] such as to enable him to make any corrections" (*Keats Circle,* I, 116), and from Keats's disavowal (which he inscribed in B. Davenport's copy, now at Harvard) of the "Advertisement" that was finally printed: "This is none of my doing—I w[as] ill at the time." The fact is, however, that Keats *did* proofread. He made corrections in the incomplete set of proof sheets of *Lamia* owned by Harvard, and early in June (perhaps on the 11th) he read and corrected proof of *The Eve of St. Agnes* after visiting his publisher John Taylor (*Letters,* II, 294–295). From 11 June to 22 June, when he suffered an attack of blood-spitting, nothing is known about his life, except that on one day (ca. 18 June) he saw Haydon, visited the British Institution, and met Thomas Monkhouse. In ten days he *could* have proofread the *Lamia* volume several times over, and his and Woodhouse's remarks about his health *could* apply to the days after the hemorrhage of 22 June.

None of the readings in the transcripts, the *Annals,* or *Lamia* can be offered as conclusive proof of Keats's own reading. With the evidence at hand it would seem that the two-part division of the printed versions deserves authority over the three-part division of the transcripts. Even if a transcript did reproduce Keats's manu-

---

[3] See W. Roberts, "Ode on a Grecian Urn," *Times Literary Supplement,* 20 August 1938, p. 544.

script accurately, one could always argue that Keats sanctioned the later change—perhaps for clarity.

II

As to critical interpretation of who says what to whom, no single explanation can satisfy the demands of text, grammar, dramatic consistency, and common sense. But critics do tend to stand on single explanations, and it may therefore be useful to summarize briefly the various possibilities, along with the objections usually raised against each.

(1) *Poet to reader:* The poet, commenting on the urn's "message," says "that is all / Ye know on earth, and all ye need to know" to the reader (and thereby to mankind generally). This is a common older interpretation which, like (2) and (3) below, is based at least initially on the *Lamia* volume's use of quotation marks to separate "Beauty . . . beauty" from the rest of the two lines. John Middleton Murry, *Keats* (London, 1955), pp. 210–226, is a typical proponent of the view. *Objections:* The reader and man have become "us" and "ours" in the final stanza; the poet's shift of address to "ye" would be both inconsistent and unprepared for (he has not earlier spoken directly to the reader/mankind). Then there is the question of meaning. At face value, the statement is false to everybody's experience of life—as one unsympathetic reader put it, "Beauty ain't truth and truth ain't beauty and you've got to know a helluva lot more than that on earth." (Critics of course have to go past face value. Victor M. Hamm, *Explicator*, III, 1945, item 56, paraphrases, "That is all you [anyone contemplating the urn] know about the urn, and all you need to know," and reads the lines as a reply to the unanswered questions posed in the first and fourth stanzas.)

The explanation by Earl R. Wasserman, *The Finer Tone* (Baltimore, 1953), p. 60, should be included under this heading: the poet's words to the reader, "that . . . know," refer not only to the urn's "message" but to the three lines preceding—"When old age. . . ." An additional objection here is the obscurity of reference, since few readers, unaided, would grasp the intended scope of "that."

(2) *Poet to urn:* This is a minority view that continues to be put forward—see William R. Wood, *English Journal,* XXIX (1940), 837–839; Roy P. Basler, *Explicator,* IV (1945), item 6; Porter Williams, Jr., *Modern Language Notes,* LXX (1955), 342–345; and especially Martin Halpern, *College English,* XXIV (1963), 284–288. The poet's final words are read as a comment on the urn's limitations: in Basler's paraphrase, "That is all you . . . know, and all you need to know; but, I know a great deal more, and a different quality of beauty and truth." *Objections:* "Ye" is normally a plural pronoun. And the urn has been referred to as "thou" throughout the poem. (Halpern cites instances of singular "ye," as well as shifts of pronouns, elsewhere in Keats's poems. A number of critics suggest that Keats may have changed pronouns to avoid the cacophony of "that is all / Thou knowest on earth, and all thou needest to know.") "On earth" in the last line is meaningless if applied to the urn.

(3) *Poet to figures on the urn:* This (proposed by G. St. Quintin, *Times Literary Supplement,* 5 February 1938, p. 92, and subsequently by Robert Berkelman, *South Atlantic Quarterly,* LVII, 1958, 354–358) is a variety of the preceding, but better accords with the normal use of "ye" as a plural. *Objections:* The figures are not "on earth." Moreover, the poet has ceased to think of them as alive and capable of hearing; he is again addressing the urn as artifact, and the images of the last stanza emphasize the lifelessness of "marble men and maidens." And there is no reason why the figures should know only "Beauty . . . beauty," or anything at all.

(4) *Urn to reader:* The commonest view of the conclusion of the ode—popularized by Cleanth Brooks and C. M. Bowra in the 1940's, reinforced by the solid stand of the Harvard Keatsians,

Douglas Bush, W. J. Bate, and David Perkins, and sometimes thought to be sanctioned by the punctuation in the transcripts (see above)—has the urn speaking the whole of the last two lines. *Objections:* There is again the question of common-sense meaning (though it seems better for the urn to tell us what we know and need to know than for the poet to do so). The principal obstacle, however, is the punctuation of the text in the *Lamia* volume. Several critics (e.g., Raymond D. Havens, *Modern Philology,* XXIV, 1926, 213; Leo Spitzer, *Comparative Literature,* VII, 1955, 220–221) have suggested that the quotation marks may have been intended to set off "Beauty . . . beauty" as an apothegm, motto, or sepulchral epigram. Bush (e.g., in his *John Keats: Selected Poems and Letters,* Boston, 1959, pp. 208, 350) and others, rejecting the *Lamia* punctuation, simply move the closing quotation mark to the end of the poem.

The Text of
Ode on Indolence

Students of Keats seem to have accepted without question the idea that Richard Monckton Milnes rearranged the stanzas of *Ode on Indolence* when he first published the poem in his *Life, Letters, and Literary Remains, of John Keats* (1848), and that H. W. Garrod restored (as he claimed) the "true order" in his most recent editions of Keats's *Poetical Works*.[1] The matter deserves correction. The order indicated by Charles Brown, in the single authoritative source of the poem, was followed exactly by Milnes and was not disturbed until Garrod took it upon himself to reorder the stanzas. The fact is that there are neither textual nor critical grounds for the current standard arrangement.

Brown's transcript (Garrod's T^2), now at Harvard, is our only manuscript version of the poem deriving from a Keats holograph, since the other extant transcript, by Richard Woodhouse (W^2), is plainly a copy of Brown's, as Woodhouse indicated by writing "from C.B." at the end. Brown transcribed the stanzas in the following order:[2]

1	One morn before me were three figures seen . . .
2	How is it, Shadows, that I knew ye not? . . .
⟨3⟩4	They faded, and, forsooth! I wanted wings . . .
⟨4⟩6	So, ye three Ghosts, adieu! Ye cannot raise . . .

[1] Oxford Standard Authors ed. (London, 1956); revised Oxford English Texts ed. (Oxford, 1958).

[2] Each first line here represents an entire stanza. Arrow brackets ($<\,>$) indicate Brown's deletions of original stanza numbers.

⟨5⟩3 A third time pass'd they by, and, passing, turn'd . . .
    5 A third time came they by;—alas! wherefore? . . .

The uncorrected "5" at the head of this final stanza is important, for it can mean but one thing—that Brown discovered a mistake and corrected the numbering of the preceding three stanzas *before* he wrote out the last stanza. Apparently he was copying from several separate sheets in Keats's holograph. When he came upon a final stanza repeating "A third time" he must have realized that something was wrong with the order of stanzas as he had thus far transcribed them. At this point, very likely in consultation with Keats, he set them right by renumbering the last three stanzas he had copied, and then wrote out the remaining stanza, which he correctly headed "5."

Brown's corrected order is thus the following:

    1 One morn before me . . .
    2 How is it, Shadows . . .
    3 A third time pass'd they by . . .
    4 They faded, and, forsooth! . . .
    5 A third time came they by . . .
    6 So, ye three Ghosts, adieu! . . .

Woodhouse copied the stanzas in this order "from C.B.," and Milnes used Brown's transcript as printer's copy for his text in the *Life* of 1848. Milnes did, however, make an unauthorized substantive change. Puzzled by the repetition of "A third time" in Brown's stanzas 3 and 5, he altered the first line of the fifth stanza to read, "And once more came they by;—alas! wherefore?" Garrod was of course aware of this change, and perhaps was unduly prejudiced against Milnes's text more generally because of it. Either forgetting or possibly never really aware of the significance of the uncorrected "5" in Brown's transcript, he seems to have formed the idea that Milnes also was responsible for changing the

order of the stanzas.[3] Incorporating a much more drastic change
than any that had occurred to Milnes, his Oxford editions give
the stanzas thus, with Brown's fifth stanza moved up to follow
stanza 2:

     I   One morn before me . . .
    II   How is it, Shadows . . .
   III   A third time came they by . . .
   IV   A third time pass'd they by . . .
    V   They faded, and, forsooth! . . .
   VI   So, ye three Ghosts, adieu! . . .

Since this "true order" that Garrod settled on has no precedent
in either of the transcripts or in Milnes's *Life,* it must have been
arrived at by some process of critical reasoning. Let us briefly consider, therefore, the argument or "action" of the poem in each
version. In Brown's corrected order it stands as follows. *Stanza 1.*
The poet sees three strange figures, who pass before him and then
come again. *Stanza 2.* He addresses them, demanding why they
are disguised as they are and why they have come to disturb his
pleasant summer indolence. *Stanza 3.* The figures pass a third
time, turn briefly to face the poet, and then fade; he desires to
follow them, recognizing them as Love, Ambition, and Poesy.
Stanza 4. The poet wants wings to pursue them, yet knows that
his desire is foolish: love, ambition, even poesy have no joys for
him; he calls for an age "shelter'd from annoy," that is, protected
from just such worldly intrusions as the figures represent. *Stanza
5.* The figures return a third time, but to no avail; luxuriating in
his mood, the poet will not be drawn out of it—" 'twas a time
[for the figures] to bid farewell!" *Stanza 6.* The poet bids the
figures adieu. In brief, the poet sees three figures, Love, Ambition,
and Poesy, who threaten his idleness; he is momentarily shaken
and longs to follow them, but then recovers himself, refuses to sur-

[3] "In T^2," he writes in his textual notes to the poem, "the numbering has
been altered to that of *1848*"; "The sense has been obscured by the placing
of the stanzas in the wrong order" (*Poetical Works,* 1958, pp. 447–448).

render his mood, and tells the figures to go away. In Garrod's arrangement, the general point is the same, but the progress is somewhat less readily graspable. With Brown's stanza 5 moved up to come between stanzas 2 and 3, the original connection between the penultimate and final stanzas is broken (" 'twas a time to bid farewell! . . . So, ye three Ghosts, adieu!"), and the poet's initial banishment of the figures is made to come *before* the account of his desire to pursue the figures and join them. Obviously the rearranged version at one time made good sense to Garrod, and it may still strike some readers (perhaps merely because they are accustomed to it) as being as reasonable as Brown's. But it cannot by any stretch of the imagination be considered so superior as to warrant a change in the order of stanzas.

There are of course obscurities in the poem, but I think not more than two. The first occurs in lines 3–5 of the second stanza:

> Was it a silent deep-disguised plot
> To steal away, and leave without a task
> My idle days?

Whether "steal away" is read as transitive ("steal away [= rob me of] . . . My idle days") or intransitive (= "tiptoe away"), the phrase "leave without a task" makes no sense in its context. Everything else in the stanza questions the figures' *interruption* of the poet's indolence; but if they came in a "deep-disguised plot" to make his days taskless, they would of course be furthering rather than disrupting the idleness that the poet wishes to maintain. The other obscurity involves the repetition of "A third time." This seems unresolvable, whether in Brown's order or Garrod's, unless one distinguishes between *passing* and *coming*. In the first stanza Keats seems to make such a distinction as he describes the figures going and then returning:

> They pass'd, like figures on a marble Urn,
> When shifted round to see the other side;

> They came again; as when the Urn once more
>   Is shifted round, the first seen Shades return.   (*T²*)

It may be that "A third time *pass'd* they by" in Brown's third stanza represents a movement in one direction, and "A third time *came* they by" in Brown's fifth represents a counter-shift or return. My general point here, though, is that neither of these obscurities is in any way helped by Garrod's or any other reordering of the stanzas.

Ode on Indolence is not in the same class with the more famous odes *To Psyche, To a Nightingale, On a Grecian Urn, On Melancholy,* and *To Autumn.* It lacks the dramatic tension that characterizes the first four, and the sharpness of imagery of all five. The poet refuses to engage in any serious conflict with Love, Ambition, and Poesy, and the poem probably genuinely reflects the indolence that is its subject. The omission of the poem from the *Lamia* volume of 1820 suggests that Keats himself recognized its inferiority (his remark to Sarah Jeffrey, 9 June 1819, that "the thing I have most enjoyed this year has been writing an ode to Indolence,"[4] does not, even if intended seriously, mean that he considered the poem a success). But even a third- or fourth-rate poem, if printed at all, deserves to have its stanzas given in the correct order, and since *Ode on Indolence* is sometimes discussed with the "great odes" and even occasionally still included *among* the "great odes" we at least ought to know what the poem was most probably intended to look like. For a proper text we must go back to Brown's transcript.

[4] *Letters,* II, 116.

Epilogue

In my lofty library study
a plaster life-mask of John Keats
(the copy owned by Amy Lowell,
propped on the bookcase behind me)
looks over my shoulder
while I write my explications.

Wearing a pirate's hat cocked
at a jaunty angle (relic of
a child's Halloween costume),
he seems quite at home
in this place, and we
have established good rapport.

"So it's true," I says,
picking up where I'd left off,
"that Madeline was only
faking her dream, knowing
all the while that Porphyro
was hiding in the closet?"

Here Keats tips me the wink,
signifying agreement. "And that
at the end of his tale
Endymion really went off
into the old oak forest
with the Indian maiden?"

Again the affable confirmation.
"What about that wretched

knight-at-arms?" "Stoned,"
he says, "the sedge
withered by his breath—and
no sedge, no birds, obviously!"

"And the philosopher Apollonius?"
"A pederast," he says, grinning,
"which explains why he was
so grumpy at Lycius' wedding,
and made the tender-personed
Lamia melt into a shade."

I turn around to my desk
to write furiously for an hour,
Keats over my shoulder
occasionally snorting, once
or twice guffawing out loud,
but not really interfering.

When I get to a hard place
he says, in friendly wise,
"Leave off this foolishness awhile."
So I go out to play tennis
with a graduate student,
whom I beat 6–2, 6–3, 6–1.

Then I return to my study,
give Keats the usual nod,
and he says, plainly
glad to see me again
and renew our conversation,
"Well, Jack, did you win?"

Index

Abercrombie, Lascelles, 123
Addison, Joseph, 125
Alison, Archibald, 156
Allen, Glen O., 14, 20, 31, 92
Ariosto, Lodovico, 93
Arnett, Carroll, 14
Arnold, Matthew, 36
Association psychology, 24, 124-126, 152, 156
Austen, Jane, 123

Bailey, Benjamin, 31, 32, 113, 151, 152; Keats's letters to, 10, 20, 21, 32, 42, 57, 69, 83, 112, 113, 119, 141, 142, 143, 151-157
Baldwin, James: *Another Country*, 46, 52
Balslev, Thora, 142
Basler, Roy P., 75, 172
Bate, Walter Jackson, 4, 34, 36, 48, 51, 62, 118, 173
Beattie, James, 156
Beddoes, Thomas Lovell: *Death's Jest-Book*, 123
Berkelman, Robert, 172
Blackstone, Bernard, 69
Blake, William, 127, 136
Blunden, Edmund, 51, 87
Boccaccio, Giovanni, 36, 38, 39, 41, 45
Bostetter, Edward E., 59

Bowra, C. M., 172
Brand, John: *Observations on Popular Antiquities*, 85
Brawne, Fanny, 96
Bridges, Robert, 15
Brooks, Cleanth, 172
Brown, Charles, 50, 98, 164, 169; transcripts of Keats's poems, 167, 168, 169, 174-178
Brown, Leonard, 15, 23
Browne, William: *Britannia's Pastorals*, 9
Burke, Edmund: *A Philosophical Enquiry into the Origin of Our Ideas of the Sublime and Beautiful*, 125
Burton, Robert: *The Anatomy of Melancholy*, 53, 77, 79, 83, 96
Bush, Douglas, 15, 18, 37, 67, 94, 95, 118, 173
Byron, George Gordon, Lord, 47; *Lara*, 122; *Manfred*, 48

Caldwell, James Ralston, 3, 151, 156
Cassirer, Ernst, 146
Chaucer, Geoffrey, 37, 93; *General Prologue*, 96; *Pardoner's Tale*, 98; *Troilus and Criseyde*, 76
Chayes, Irene H., 60, 61
Clarke, Charles Cowden, 9
Clarke, John, 99, 100

Coleridge, Samuel Taylor, 130, 145, 152; *Biographia Literaria*, 126, 129-130, 149, 152; *Christabel*, 49, 122; *Dejection: An Ode*, 124, 129; *The Eolian Harp*, 102; *Kubla Khan*, 23; *The Rime of the Ancient Mariner*, 23, 102; *This Lime-Tree Bower My Prison*, 155; *To William Wordsworth*, 130
Colvin, Sidney, 15, 36, 76
Conder, Josiah, 4
Creative sensibility (Wordsworth and Coleridge), 105, 127-135, 139, 141, 143-144, 153, 155

Dante Alighieri: *Inferno*, 87
D'Avanzo, Mario L., 15
Davenport, B., 170
Dilke, Charles Wentworth, 167, 168
Donne, John: *The Canonization*, 79
Dreams, dreaming, 20-21, 33-35, 46, 47, 52-54, 59-60, 61, 62, 63-64, 69-70, 72, 84-93, 97, 111-113, 115-116, 141, 163

Eliot, George, 94
Eliot, T. S., 147
Elmes, James, 169
Evert, Walter H., 15, 18, 48, 49-50, 57, 59, 65-66, 151

Fairy-tale imagery, 73, 88-89, 91, 116
Fielding, Henry, 32, 113
Finney, Claude Lee, 15, 36, 78, 136-137
Florio, John, 36
Foakes, R. A., 69, 79
Fogle, R. H., 68
Ford, Newell F., 15, 151, 153
Forman, H. Buxton, 75
Frye, Northrop, 15, 101, 123

Garrod, H. W., 8, 118, 158, 159, 161, 162, 164, 174, 175-176, 177, 178
Gérard, Albert, 14, 25, 34, 123
Gittings, Robert, 96
Godfrey, Clarisse, 14

Halpern, Martin, 172
Hamm, Victor M., 171
Hartley, David, 24, 124, 126, 127, 135, 143, 156; *Observations on Man*, 125, 126
Havens, Raymond D., 173
Haworth, Helen E., 15
Haydon, Benjamin Robert, 11, 87, 169, 170; Keats's letters to, 32, 33, 49, 50
Hazlitt, William, 36, 44
Heffernan, James A. W., 127
Hessey, James Augustus, 51, 87
Hewlett, Dorothy, 3-4
Hobbes, Thomas: *Leviathan*, 125, 126, 153
Hopkins, Gerard Manley: *Hurrahing in Harvest*, 130
Houghton, Walter E., 94, 98
Hume, David: *Philosophical Essays Concerning Human Understanding*, 133
Hunt, Leigh, 6, 44, 76, 85, 117, 138, 139; *Politics and Poetics*, 136-138

Imagination, 105, 114, 118-119, 125-126; naturalized, 100, 126-135, 141, 143-146, 152, 154, 156; visionary, 20-21, 24-26, 31, 34-35, 52-53, 69-70, 71, 88, 92, 100, 105, 107, 112-113, 115-116, 118, 127, 135-141, 143-147, 151-157

Jeffrey, Sarah, 178
Johnson, Samuel, 123; *Rasselas*, 118
Jonson, Ben, 85, 100

Keats, George, 10, 32, 114, 159, 167, 168

Keats, John: *Bards of Passion and of Mirth*, 116; *La Belle Dame sans Merci*, 2, 52, 54, 89, 91, 115, 116; *Bright star*, 55, 103-104; *Calidore*, 7; *Endymion*, 7, 10, 12, 13, 14-23, 25-26, 28, 29, 30, 31, 33, 46, 47, 49-50, 51, 53, 54, 55, 57, 65, 70, 72, 99, 102, 111-113, 114, 119, 123, 141, 153-154, 156-157; *The Eve of St. Agnes*, 2, 20, 37, 45, 51, 52, 54, 55, 56, 66, 67-87, 88-89, 91, 93, 97, 115, 116, 158-166, 170; *The Eve of Saint Mark*, 47, 51, 89, 94-98, 115; *The Fall of Hyperion*, 46, 47, 51, 59-64, 90, 115, 141; *Fancy*, 2, 116; *Four Seasons fill the Measure of the year*, 33, 92; *God of the Meridian*, 33, 92; *Great spirits now on earth are sojourning*, 11; *Had I a man's fair form*, 54; *How many bards gild the lapses of time*, 10; *Hyperion*, 37, 46, 47-52, 53, 54, 59, 60, 64, 65, 66, 114, 116, 117; *Imitation of Spenser*, 4, 8; *In a drear-nighted December*, 33; *Isabella*, 31, 33, 35-45, 50, 51, 55, 57, 67, 73, 114, 116; *I stood tip-toe*, 4, 6-7, 8, 11, 12, 13, 70, 111, 138-139, 140, 142; *Keen, fitful gusts are whisp'ring*, 10, 11; *Lamia*, 2, 46, 47, 52-59, 60, 65, 89-90, 91, 96, 97, 115, 116, 141; *Lines on the Mermaid Tavern*, 33, 116, 169; *Lines Written in the Highlands*, 92, 114; *Ode on a Grecian Urn*, 2, 52, 57, 90-91, 97, 104, 107-109, 115, 116, 118, 167-173, 178; *Ode on Indolence*, 104-105, 174-178; *Ode on Melancholy*, 2, 38, 47, 52, 55, 88, 90, 104, 109-

110, 115, 116, 117, 178; *Ode to a Nightingale*, 2, 52, 54, 57, 90-91, 97, 104, 106-107, 108, 115, 116, 118, 136, 138, 141, 169, 170, 178; *Ode to May*, 44; *Ode to Psyche*, 2, 5, 52, 55, 104-106, 115, 116-117, 139, 148, 178; *On a Dream*, 87; *On First Looking into Chapman's Homer*, 4, 10-11; *On Leaving Some Friends at an Early Hour*, 11; *On Receiving a Curious Shell*, 7, 8; *On Receiving a Laurel Crown from Leigh Hunt*, 8; *On Sitting Down to Read King Lear Once Again*, 12, 32-33, 37, 92, 113; *On the Grasshopper and Cricket*, 11; *On Visiting the Tomb of Burns*, 114; *O Solitude*, 4; *Otho the Great*, 2; *Robin Hood*, 33, 116, 117; *Sleep and Poetry*, 4, 8, 11-13, 32, 46, 62, 111, 139, 140, 142; *Specimen of an Induction*, 7; *Spenser! a jealous honourer of thine*, 33; *This pleasant tale is like a little copse*, 44; *To * * * ** (Mary Frogley), 8; *To Autumn*, 2, 64, 104, 110, 115, 116, 117, 178; *To Charles Cowden Clarke*, 9, 10, 12; *To George Felton Mathew*, 8, 9, 12, 137; *To Hope*, 4, 8, 13; *To J. H. Reynolds, Esq.*, 31, 33-36, 37, 44, 50, 62, 83-84, 92, 108, 113-114; *To Leigh Hunt, Esq.*, 5-6, 13, 105; *To My Brother George* (epistle), 8, 9-10, 12, 111, 139-140; *To My Brothers*, 10; *To Some Ladies*, 4, 7, 13; *Welcome joy, and welcome sorrow*, 33, 55; *When I have fears*, 33; *Woman! when I behold thee*, 4, 8, 13; *Written in Disgust of Vulgar Superstition*, 84, 95; *Written on*

Keats, John (*continued*)
the Day that Mr. Leigh Hunt
Left Prison, 4, 10
Keats, Tom, 32, 50, 114

Lamb, Charles, 36
Langbaum, Robert, 127
Locke, John, 24, 124, 126, 127, 135,
143, 151, 156; *An Essay Concerning Humane Understanding*,
125, 133
Lowell, Amy, 15, 87, 118, 158, 162

Mathew, George Felton, 3-4, 7, 9
Maxwell, J. C., 114
Melville, Herman, 83, 84
Miller, Bruce E., 15, 19
Milnes, Richard Monckton, 117,
174, 175, 176
Milton, John: *Paradise Lost*, 20, 64,
77, 81, 112, 153
Modern Romanticism, 6, 146, 148-
149
Monkhouse, Thomas, 170
Moore, Marianne, 147
Murry, John Middleton, 15, 55, 63,
142, 171

Negative Capability, 16, 32, 118,
152
Newton, Sir Isaac, 124, 134

Owen, F. M., 14

Patterson, Charles I., Jr., 53
Peckham, Morse, 123
Perkins, David, 53, 92, 103, 105,
173
Pleasure-pain complexity of life,
55-56, 62-63, 88, 90, 93, 109-110,
115
Pope, Alexander, 100
Priestley, F. E. L., 36, 37, 76

Priestley, Joseph: *Hartley's Theory
of the Human Mind*, 125-126,
138, 153

Religion, 84, 96; religious lan-
guage, 72-73, 164-165
Reynolds, John Hamilton, 36, 44;
Keats's letters to, 44, 50, 64, 71,
92, 141
Richardson, Samuel: *Clarissa*, 78-79
Riddel, Joseph N., 146
Ridley, M. R., 36, 55
Roberts, W., 170
Rollins, Hyder E., 36, 164
Romance, 31-33, 37, 41, 43, 44, 45,
67, 69, 113, 116
Romanticism, 29, 101, 103, 105, 120-
126, 145-149

St. Quintin, G., 172
Scott, Sir Walter, 32
Selincourt, Ernest de, 3, 4, 15, 49
Severn, Joseph, 164
Severs, J. Burke, 54
Shakespeare, William, 32, 50, 100,
113; *Cymbeline*, 78; *Hamlet*, 86;
King Lear, 12; *Romeo and
Juliet*, 73, 76
Shelley, Percy Bysshe, 23, 29, 48,
127, 136, 157; *Alastor*, 17, 23-25,
26, 28, 29, 111, 133; *Epipsychi-
dion*, 122; "On Love," 24; *Prome-
theus Unbound*, 48, 52, 123
Simons, Hi, 14, 29
Slote, Bernice, 87
Smollett, Tobias, 32, 113
Sotheby, William: translation of
Wieland's *Oberon*, 76
Spenser, Edmund, 4, 7, 8, 33;
Muiopotmos, 3
Sperry, Stuart M., Jr., 15, 20, 34,
64, 86
Spitzer, Leo, 173

Steele, Mabel A. E., 95, 161
Stevens, Wallace, 14, 26, 29, 146-148, 149; *The Comedian as the Letter C,* 14, 26-29; *Of Modern Poetry,* 119; *Sunday Morning,* 149
Stroup, Thomas B., 78
Swinburne, Algernon Charles, 78

Taylor, John, 81, 159, 162-163, 164, 170; Keats's letters to, 16, 17, 101
Tennyson, Alfred, 100
Thorpe, Clarence D., 15, 118, 142

Vision, visionary experience, 6, 8, 12, 59, 111, 115, 138-140. *See also* Imagination

Ward, Aileen, 36, 37, 38, 98
Wasserman, Earl R., 20, 69, 71, 72, 123, 151, 171
Whitley, Alvin, 167
Wicker, Brian, 61
Wieland, Christoph Martin: *Oberon,* 76
Wigod, Jacob D., 14, 15, 18, 167
Wilkie, Brian, 48
Williams, Porter, Jr., 172
Williams, William Carlos, 147, 149

Wizard of Oz, The (film version), 102
Wood, William R., 172
Woodhouse, Richard, 36, 57, 63, 81, 83, 87, 90, 159-161, 162, 163, 164, 170; transcripts of Keats's poems, 63, 81, 159, 161, 167, 168, 174, 175
Wordsworth, William, 31, 32, 43, 44, 47, 50, 113, 122, 124, 127-135, 142-145, 148, 149, 152, 153, 155; *Elegiac Stanzas,* 1-2, 143; *The Excursion,* 142, 153, 163; *Expostulation and Reply,* 1; *I wandered lonely as a cloud,* 47, 144; *Lyrical Ballads,* Preface, 1, 43; *A narrow girdle of rough stones,* 102; *Ode: Intimations of Immortality,* 1-2, 23, 102; *Peter Bell,* 8, 102, 143, 148; *The Prelude,* 110, 118-119, 124, 127-129, 130-135, 142-143, 144, 145, 148; *The Recluse,* 135; *Resolution and Independence,* 102; *A slumber did my spirit seal,* 102, 121-122; *The Solitary Reaper,* 47; *The Thorn,* 43; *Tintern Abbey,* 23, 102, 133, 144, 152, 153; *To H. C.,* 35; *A whirl-blast from behind the hill,* 139
Wright, Herbert G., 36, 43, 87

About the Author

Jack Stillinger, professor of English at the University of Illinois, holds degrees from the University of Texas (1953), Northwestern (1954), and Harvard (1958). He has published seven earlier books, beginning with *The Early Draft of John Stuart Mill's "Autobiography"* (1961), and many articles, reviews, and poems. For the last half-dozen years he has been principal editor of the *Journal of English and Germanic Philology,* and for the last three has been director of the graduate programs in English at Illinois. In 1964–65 he held a Guggenheim fellowship. In the spring of 1970 he was elected to a permanent professorship in the University of Illinois Center for Advanced Study.